48 CLASSIC TUNES
FROM 33 DISNEY MOVIES & SHOWS

ISBN 0-634-00065-9

Walt Disney Music Company
Wonderland Music Company, Inc.

DISTRIBUTED BY

HAL•LEONARD®
CORPORATION
7777 W. BLUEMOUND RD. P.O. BOX 13819 MILWAUKEE, WI 53213

Visit Hal Leonard Online at
www.halleonard.com

CONTENTS

THE AGE OF NOT BELIEVING

from Walt Disney's BEDKNOBS AND BROOMSTICKS

Words and Music by RICHARD M. SHERMAN
and ROBERT B. SHERMAN

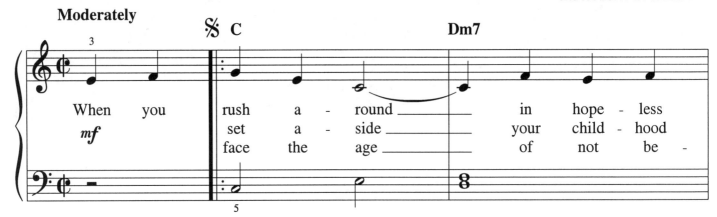

When you rush a - round _____ in hope - less
set a - side _____ your child - hood
face the age _____ of not be -

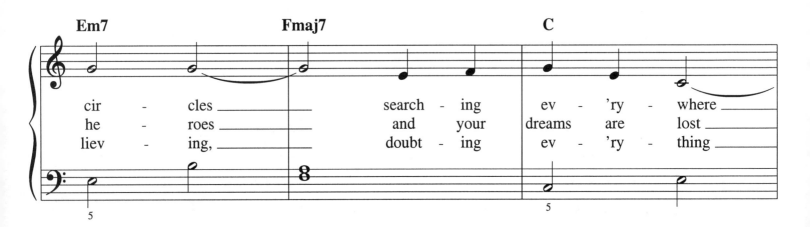

cir - cles _____ search - ing ev - 'ry - where _____
he - roes _____ and your dreams are lost _____
liev - ing, _____ doubt - ing ev - 'ry - thing _____

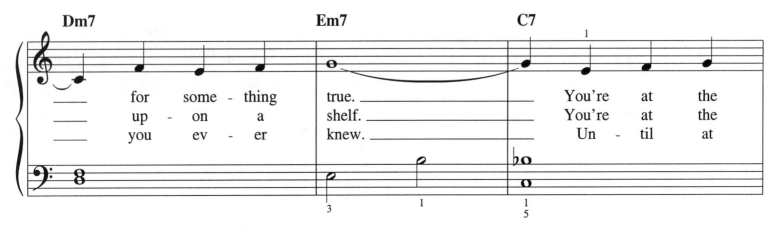

for some - thing true. _____ You're at the
up - on a shelf. _____ You're at the
you ev - er knew. _____ Un - til at

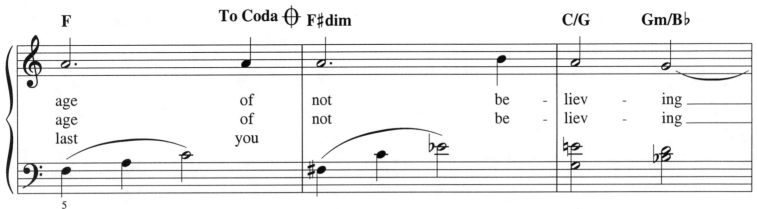

age of not be - liev - ing _____
age of not be - liev - ing _____
last you

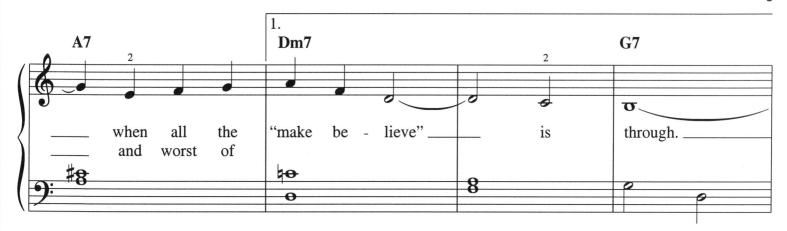

A7 ... **Dm7** ... **G7**

when all the "make be - lieve" _____ is through. _____
and worst of

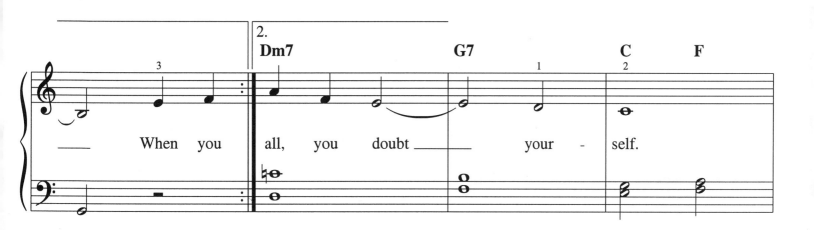

Dm7 ... **G7** ... **C** ... **F**

When you all, you doubt _____ your - self.

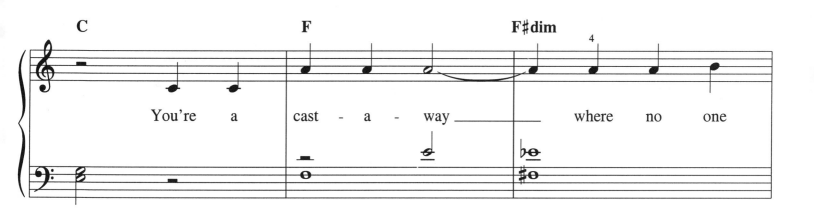

C ... **F** ... **F♯dim**

You're a cast - a - way _____ where no one

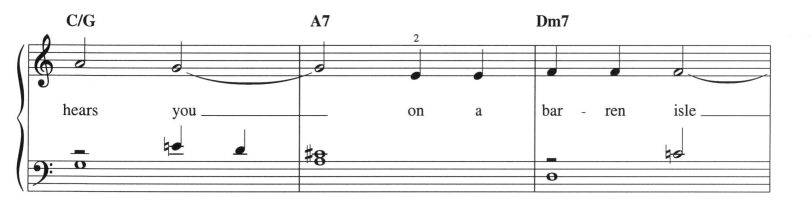

C/G ... **A7** ... **Dm7**

hears you _____ on a bar - ren isle _____

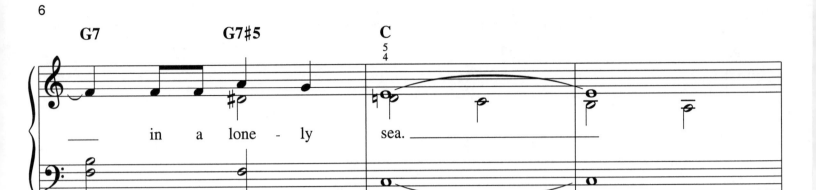

in a lone - ly sea. _____

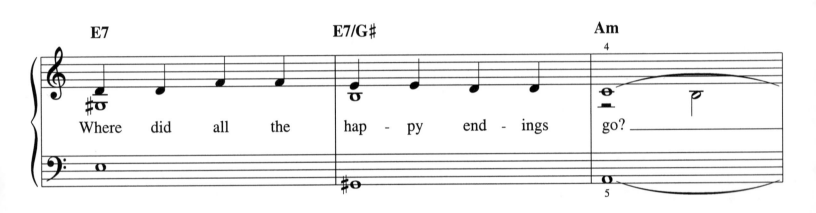

Where did all the hap - py end - ings go? _____

Where can all the good times be? _____

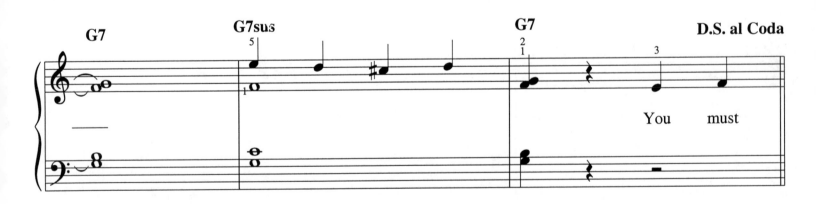

You must

CODA

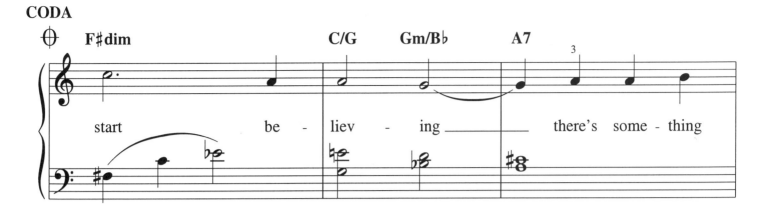

start be - liev - ing _____ there's some - thing

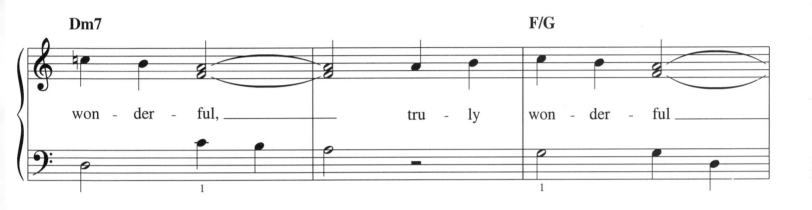

won - der - ful, _____ tru - ly won - der - ful _____

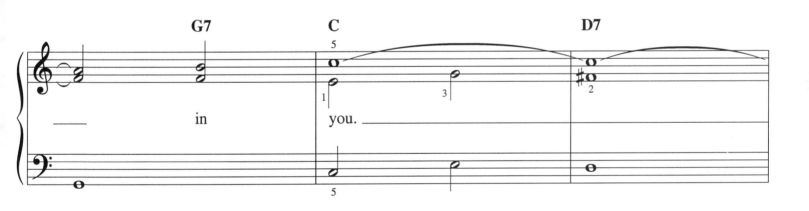

_____ in you. _____

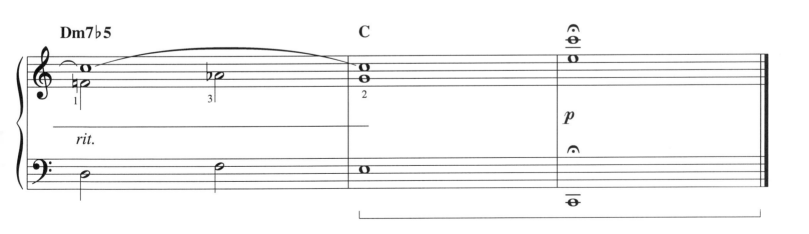

rit.

p

ALICE IN WONDERLAND
from Walt Disney's ALICE IN WONDERLAND

Words by BOB HILLIARD
Music by SAMMY FAIN

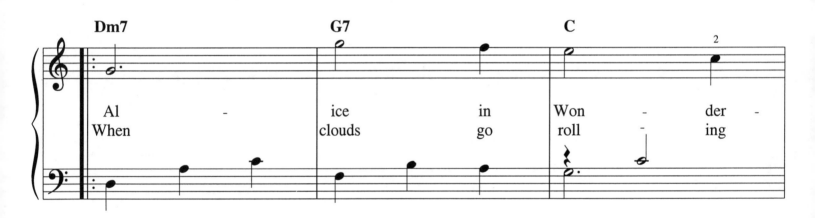

Al - ice in Won - der -
When clouds go roll - ing

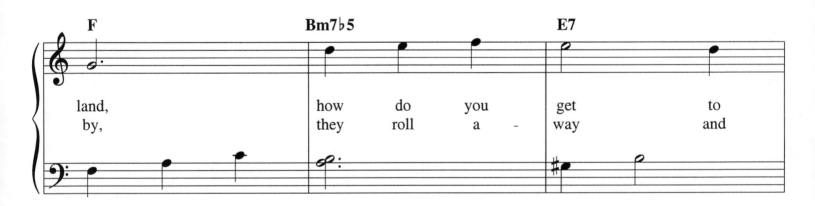

land, how do you get to
by, they roll a - way and

9

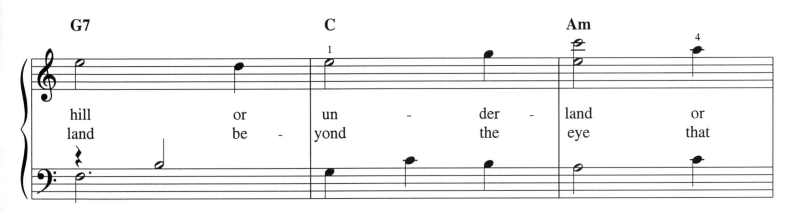

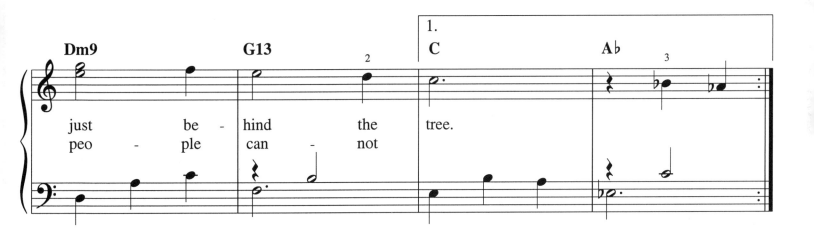

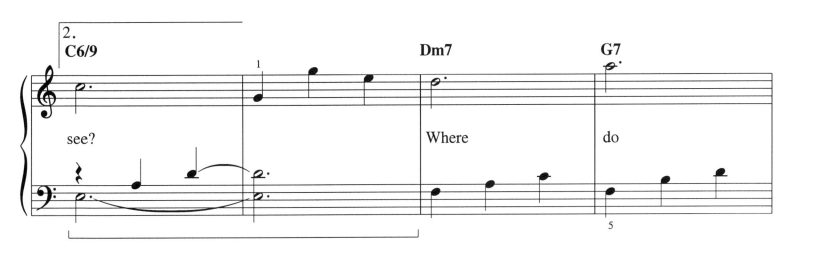

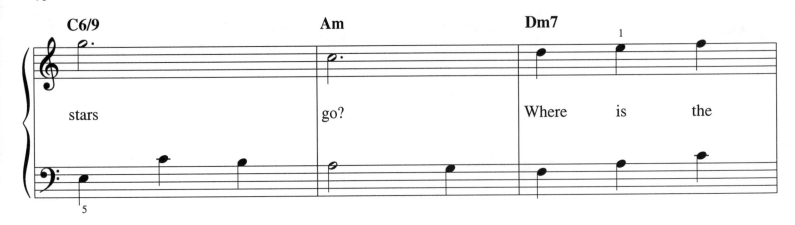

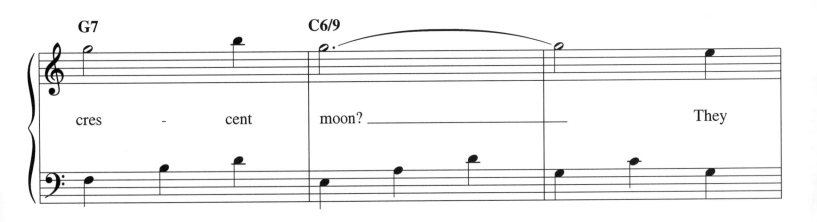

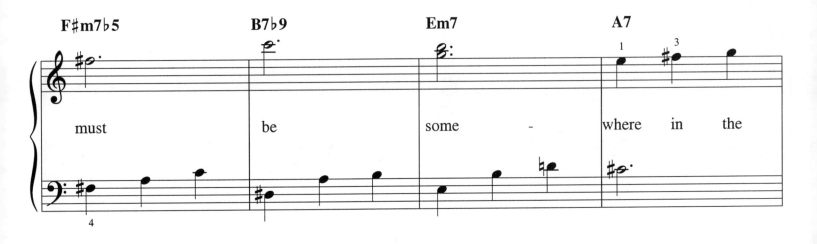

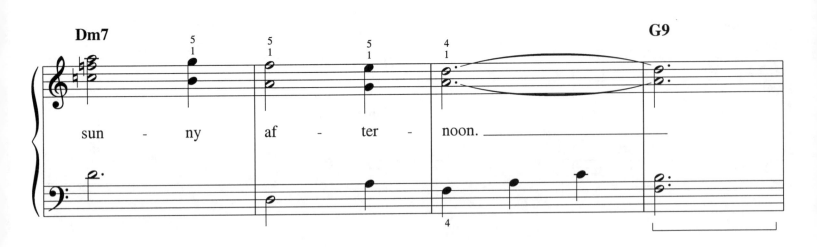

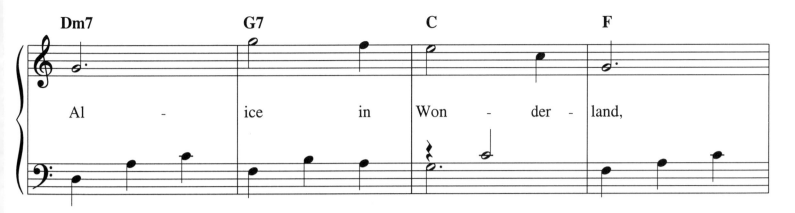

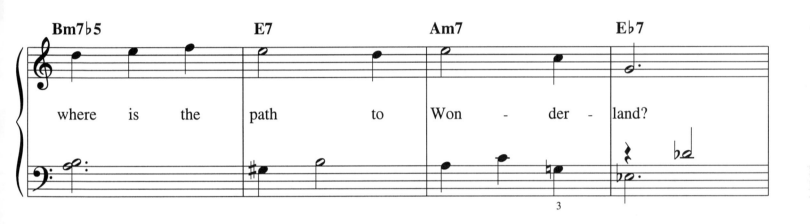

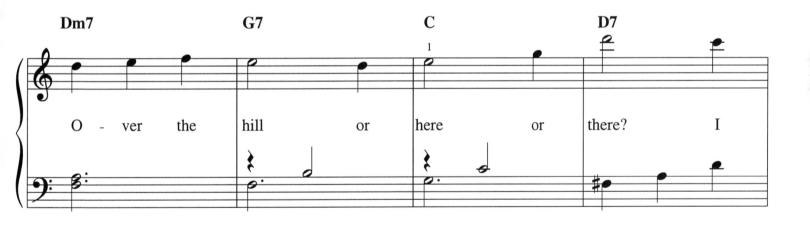

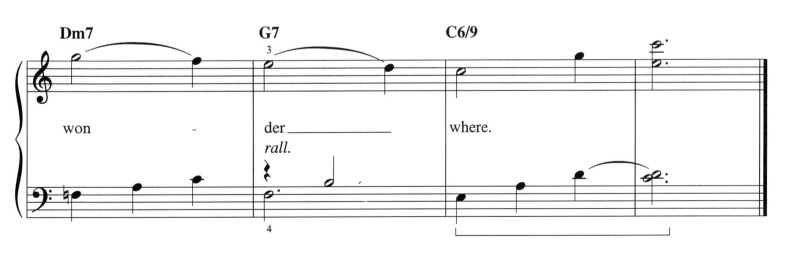

ARABIAN NIGHTS
from Walt Disney's ALADDIN

Lyrics by HOWARD ASHMAN
Music by ALAN MENKEN

Moderately

Oh, I come from a land, from a

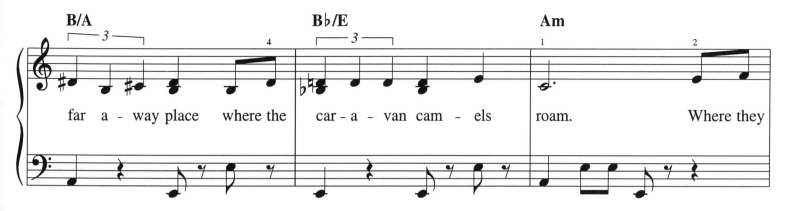

far a - way place where the car - a - van cam - els roam. Where they

cut off your ear if they don't like your face. It's bar- bar - ic, but hey, it's

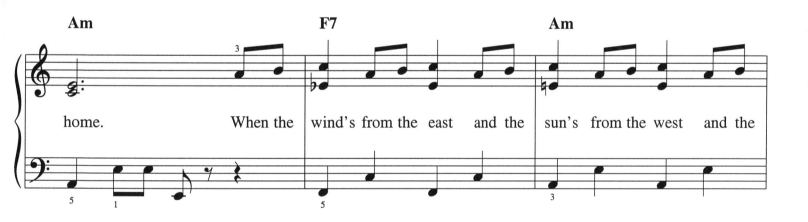

home. When the wind's from the east and the sun's from the west and the

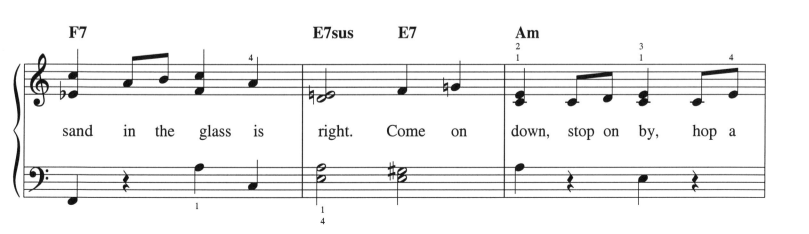

sand in the glass is right. Come on down, stop on by, hop a

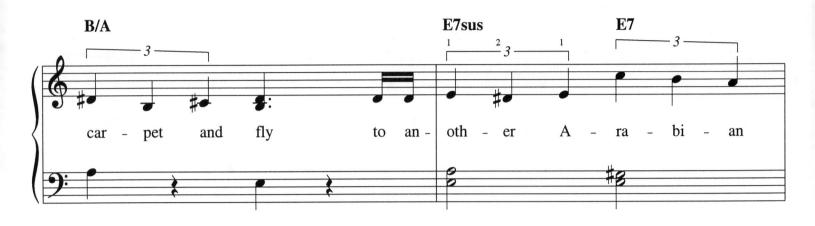

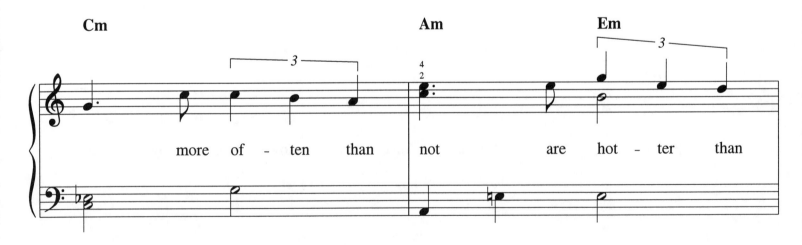

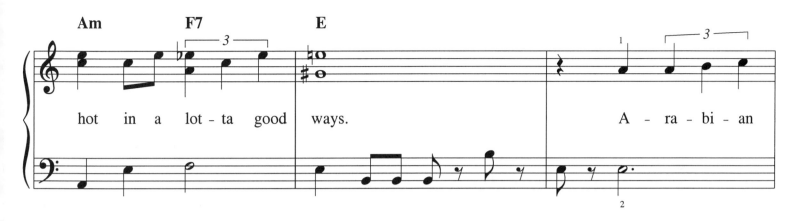

hot in a lot-ta good ways.

A - ra - bi - an

nights

'neath A - ra - bi - an

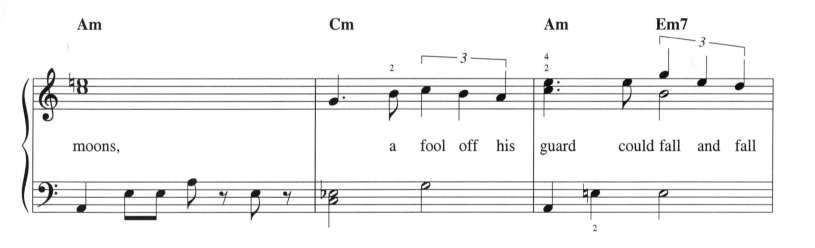

moons,

a fool off his guard could fall and fall

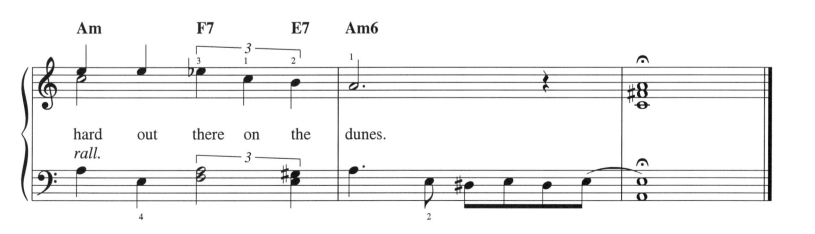

hard out there on the dunes.

rall.

THE ARISTOCATS
from Walt Disney's THE ARISTOCATS

Words and Music by RICHARD M. SHERMAN
and ROBERT B. SHERMAN

Which pets' ad - dress is the fin - est in Pa -
Which pets are blessed with the fair - est in forms and

ree? Which pets pos - sess the
faces? Which pets know best all the

long - est ped - i - gree? Which pets
gen - tle so - cial graces? Which pets

get to sleep on vel - vet mats?
live on cream and lov - ing pats?

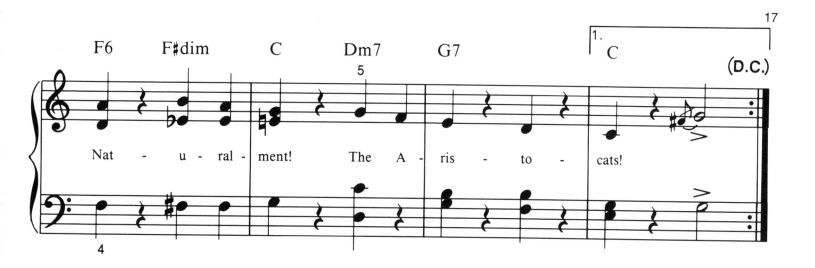

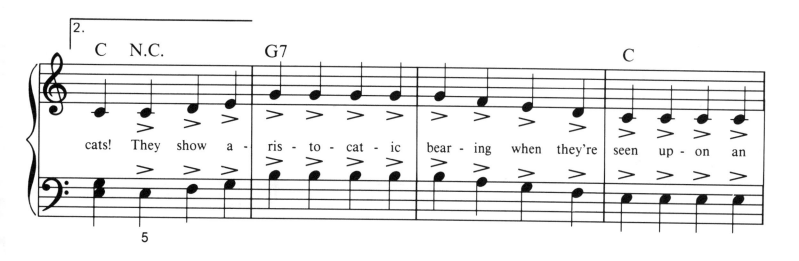

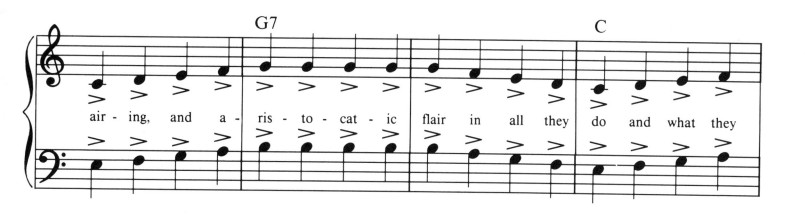

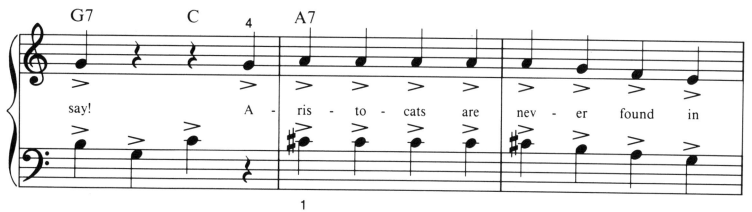

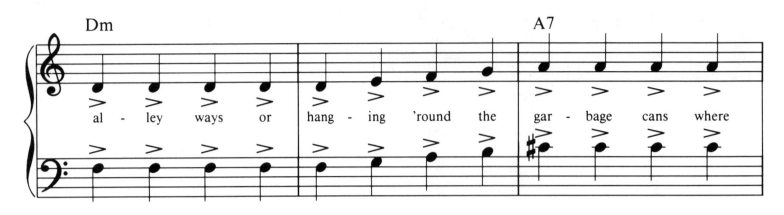

al - ley ways or hang - ing 'round the gar - bage cans where

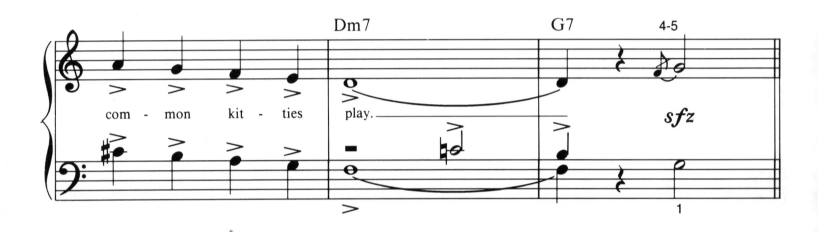

com - mon kit - ties play.

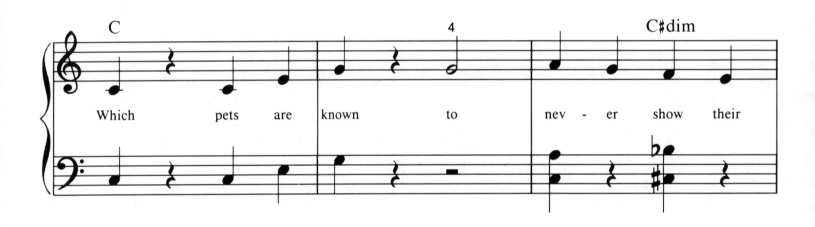

Which pets are known to nev - er show their

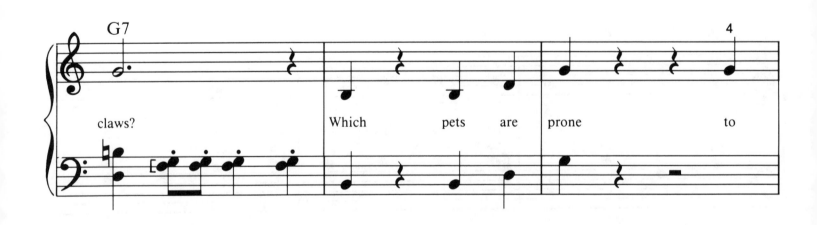

claws? Which pets are prone to

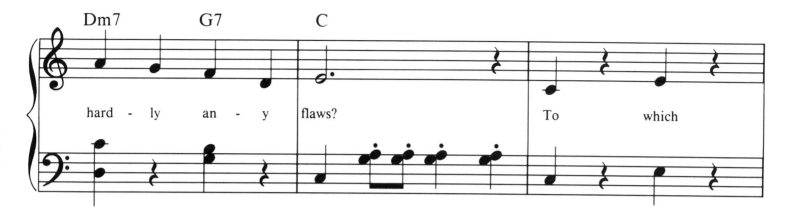
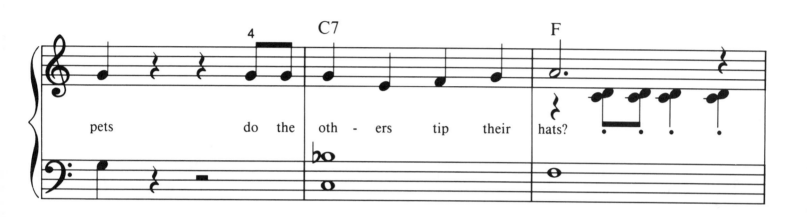
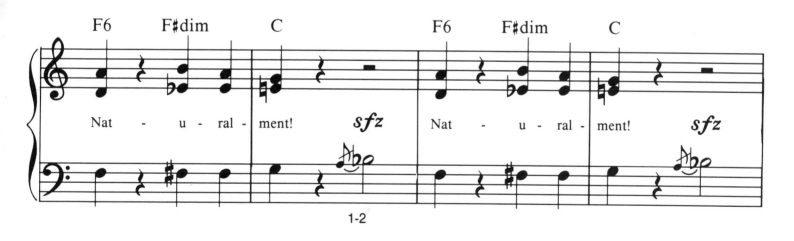
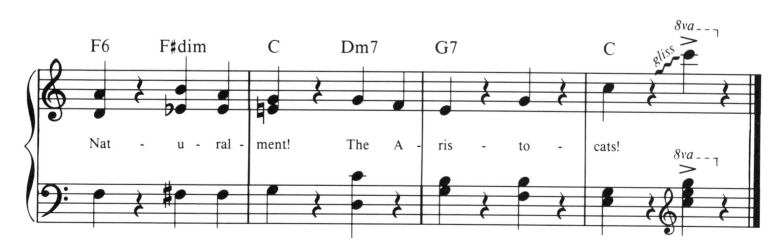

THE BARE NECESSITIES
from Walt Disney's THE JUNGLE BOOK

Words and Music by
TERRY GILKYSON

Look for the bare ne - ces - si - ties, the sim - ple bare ne -

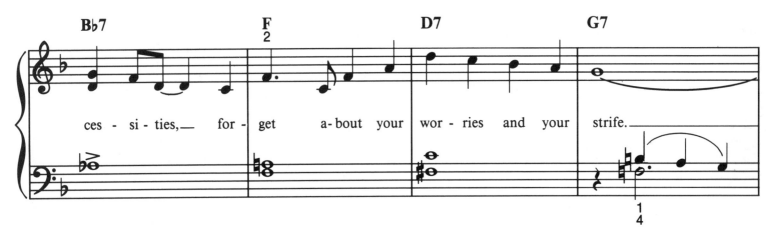

ces - si - ties,— for - get a - bout your wor - ries and your strife.

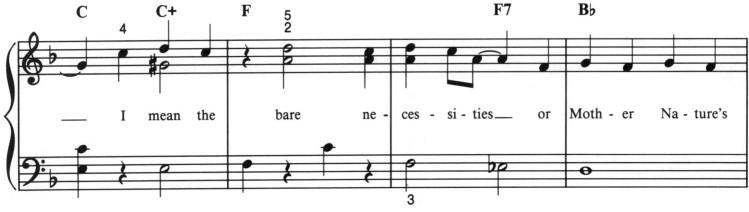

I mean the bare ne - ces - si - ties— or Moth - er Na - ture's

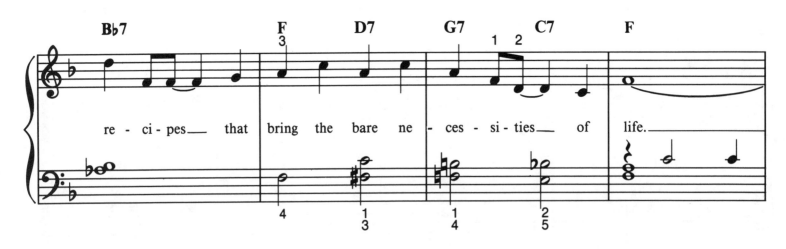

re - ci - pes— that bring the bare ne - ces - si - ties— of life.

21

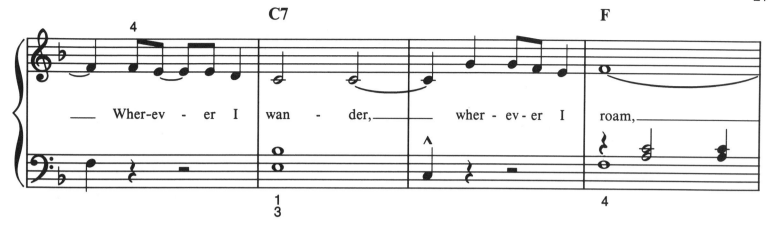

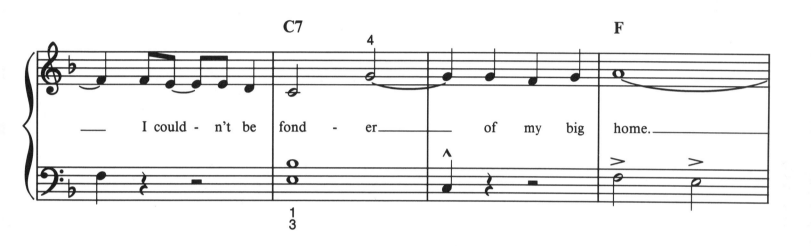

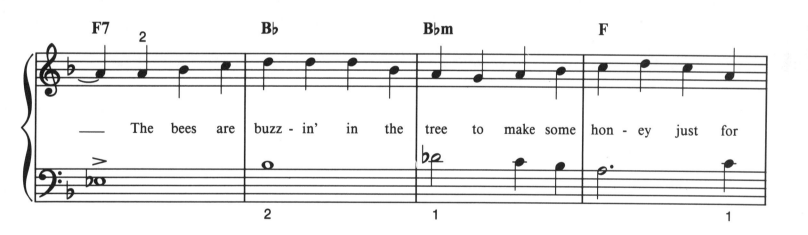

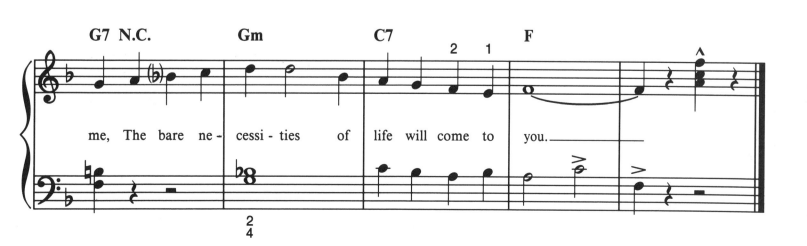

BE OUR GUEST
from Walt Disney's BEAUTY AND THE BEAST

Lyrics by HOWARD ASHMAN
Music by ALAN MENKEN

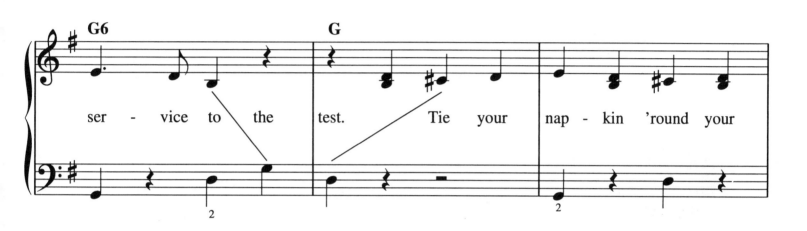

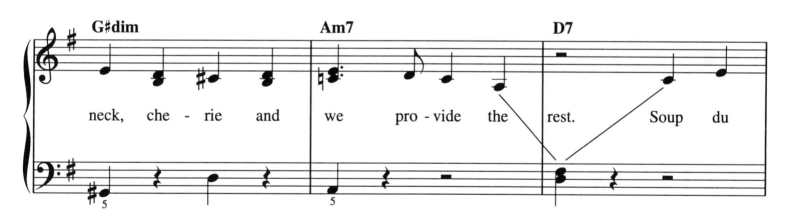

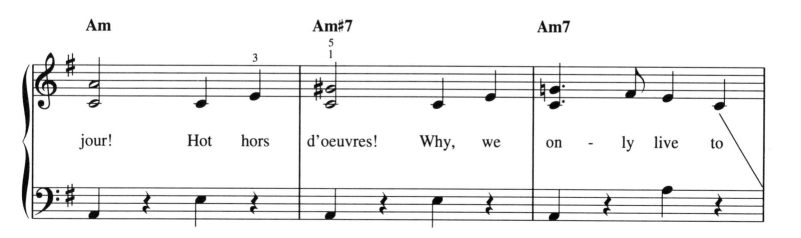

24

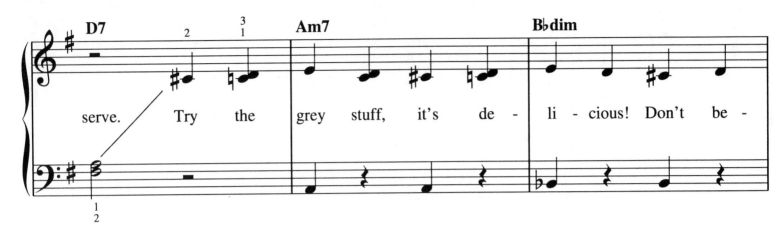

serve. Try the grey stuff, it's de - li - cious! Don't be -

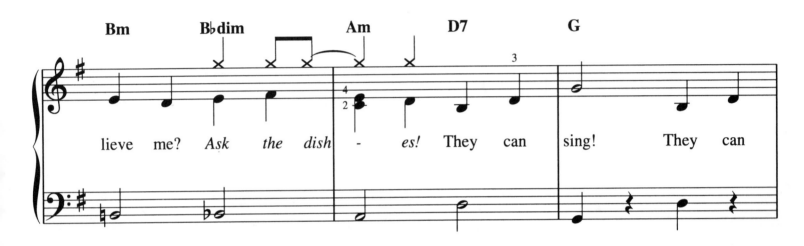

lieve me? *Ask the dish - es!* They can sing! They can

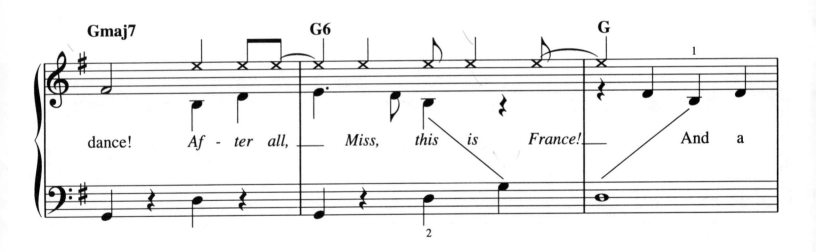

dance! *Af - ter all,* ___ *Miss, this is France!* ___ And a

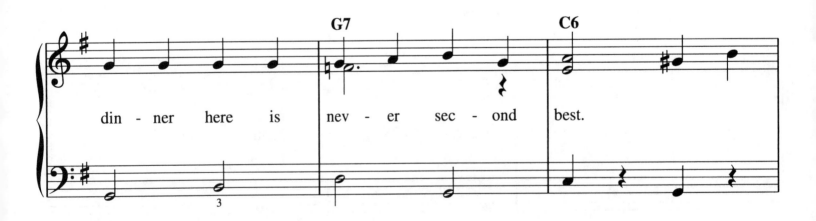

din - ner here is nev - er sec - ond best.

25

Go on, un - fold your men - u, take a

glance, and then ___ you'll be our guest, *oui,* our

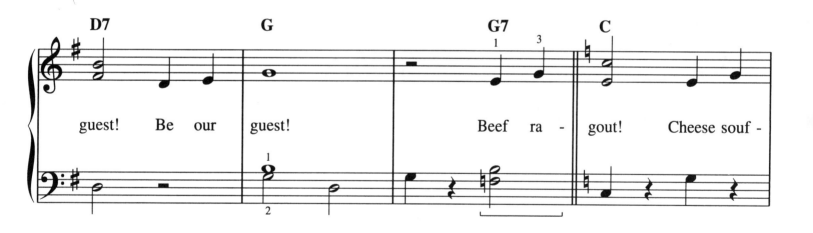

guest! Be our guest! Beef ra - gout! Cheese souf -

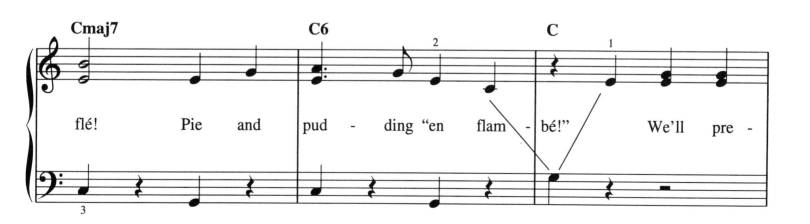

flé! Pie and pud - ding "en flam - bé!" We'll pre -

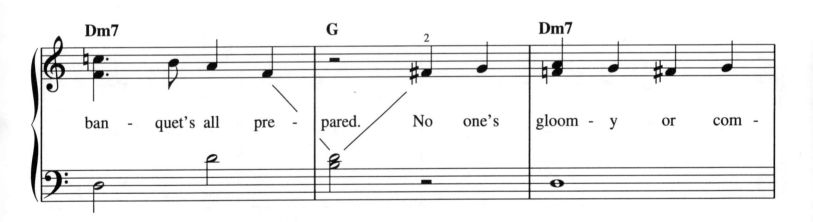

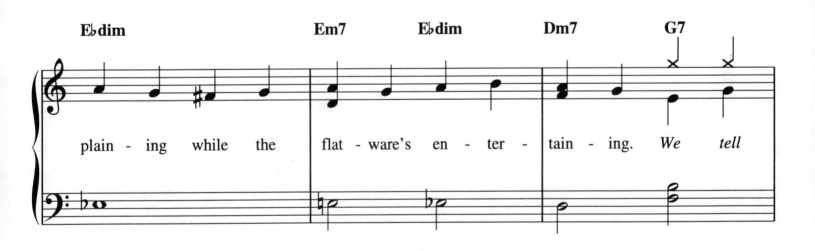

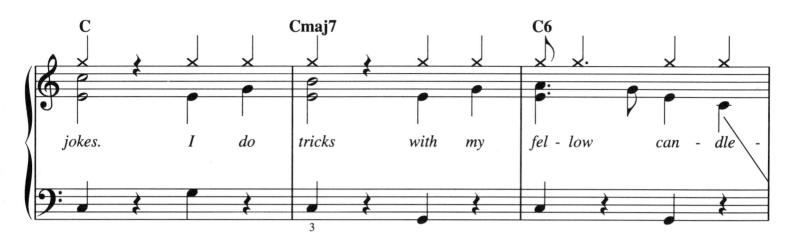

jokes.   *I*   *do*   *tricks*   *with*   *my*   *fel - low*   *can - dle -*

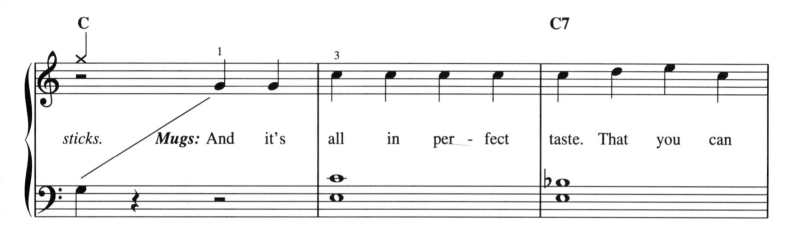

sticks.   ***Mugs:*** And   it's   all   in   per - fect   taste.   That   you   can

bet!   ***All:*** Come   on   and   lift   your   glass

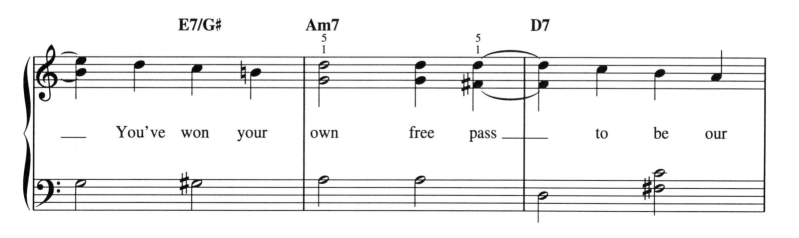

You've   won   your   own   free   pass   to   be   our

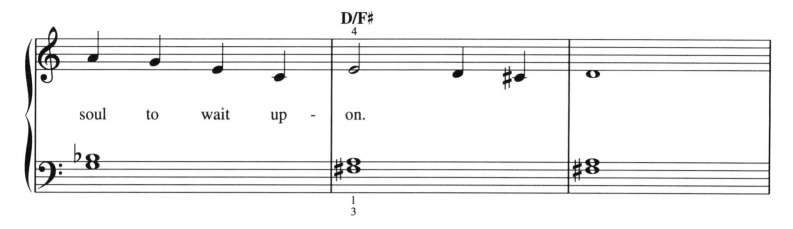

soul to wait up - on.

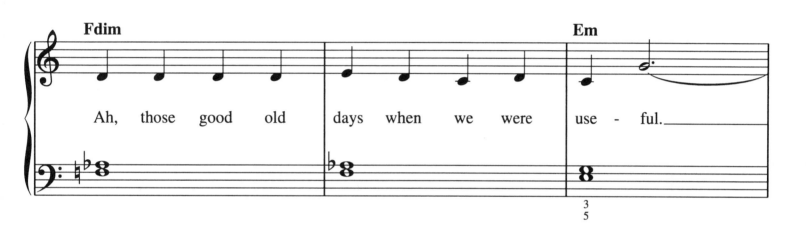

Ah, those good old days when we were use - ful._____

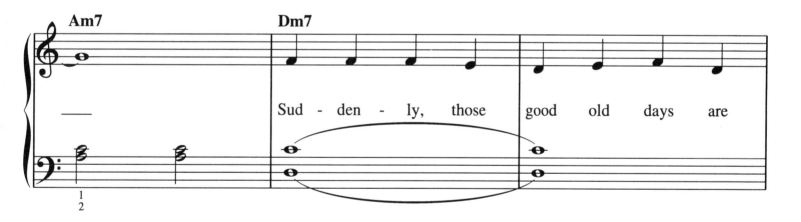

_____ Sud - den - ly, those good old days are

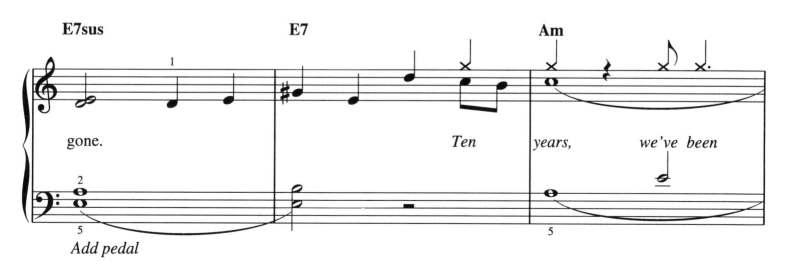

gone. *Ten years, we've been*

Add pedal

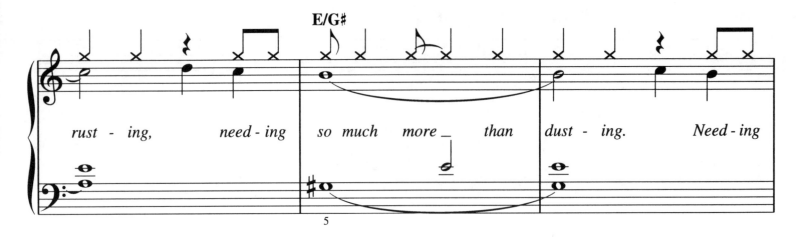

rust - ing, need - ing so much more _ than dust - ing. Need - ing

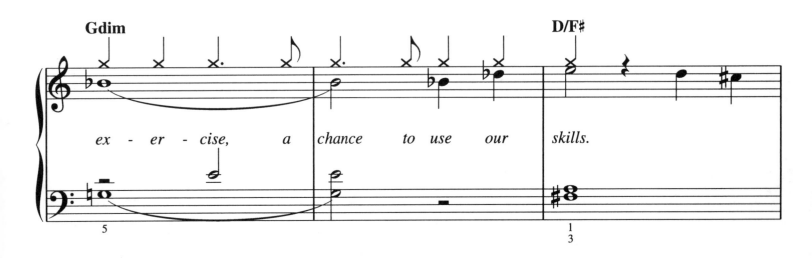

ex - er - cise, a chance to use our skills.

Most days, we just lay a - round the

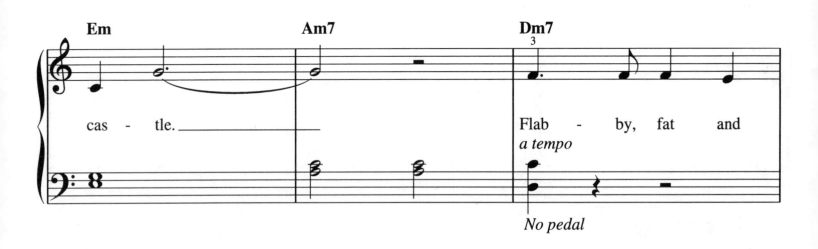

cas - tle. _____ Flab - by, fat and

a tempo

No pedal

31

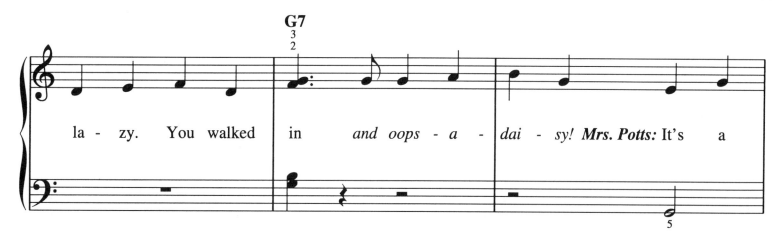

la - zy. You walked in *and oops - a - dai - sy!* **Mrs. Potts:** It's a

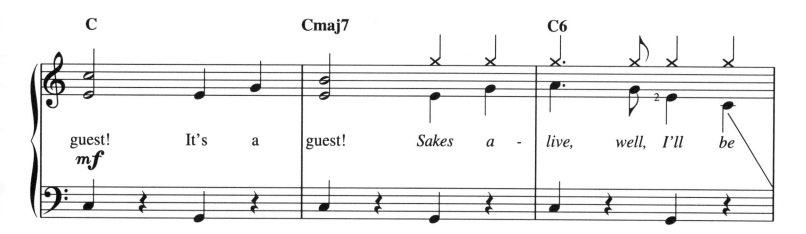

guest! It's a guest! *Sakes a - live, well, I'll be*

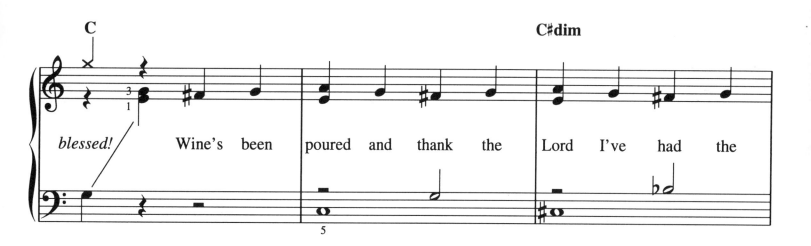

blessed! Wine's been poured and thank the Lord I've had the

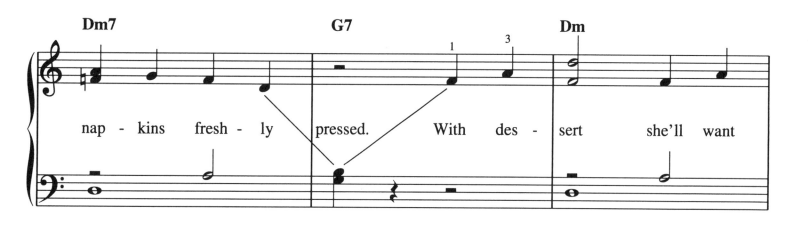

nap - kins fresh - ly pressed. With des - sert she'll want

tea.   *And   my*   *dear,   that's   fine   with   me.*   While   the

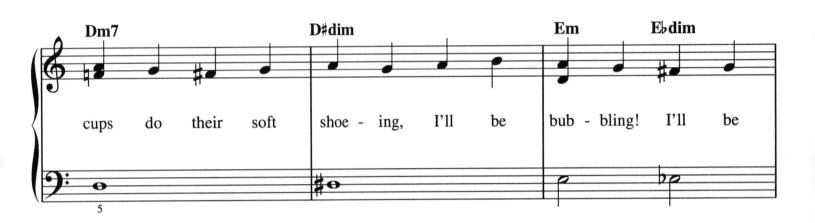

cups   do   their   soft   shoe - ing,   I'll   be   bub - bling!   I'll   be

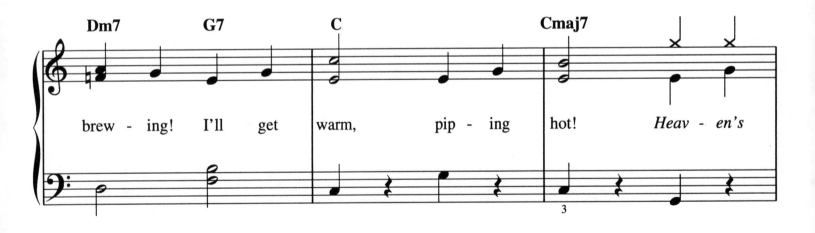

brew - ing!   I'll   get   warm,   pip - ing   hot!   *Heav - en's*

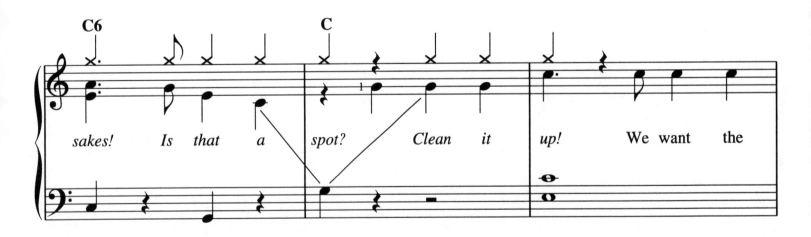

sakes!   *Is   that   a*   *spot?*   *Clean   it*   *up!*   We   want   the

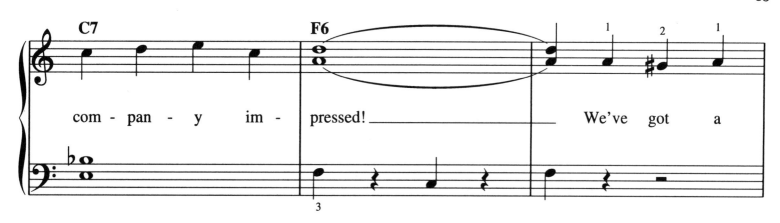

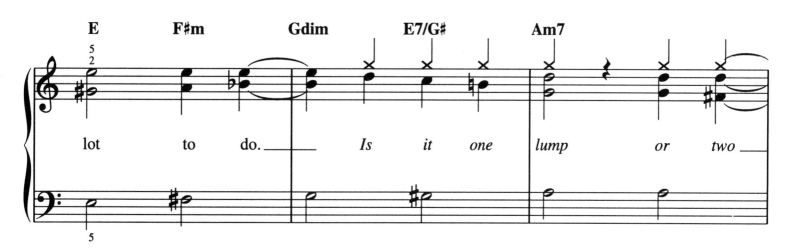

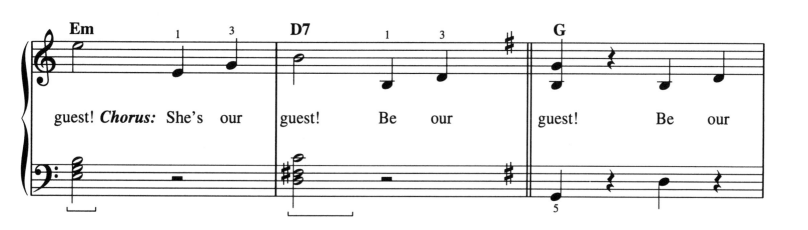

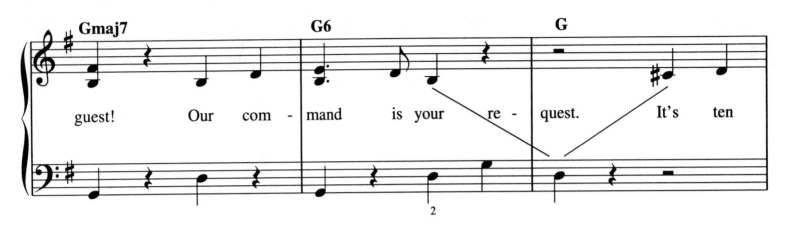

guest! Our com - mand is your re - quest. It's ten

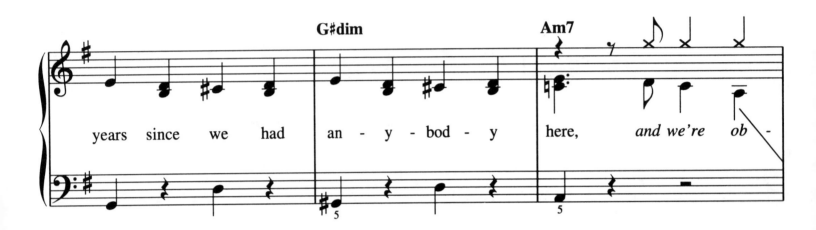

years since we had an - y - bod - y here, *and we're ob -*

sessed. With your meal, with your ease, yes, in -

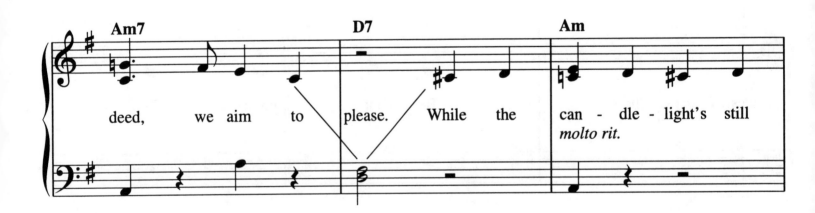

deed, we aim to please. While the can - dle - light's still
molto rit.

glow - ing let us help you, we'll keep go - ing course by

course, one by one! 'Til you shout, "E - nough. I'm

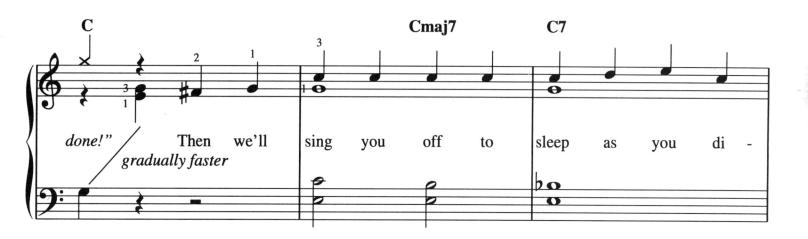

done!" Then we'll sing you off to sleep as you di -

gest. To - night you'll prop your feet

36

Gdim   **E7/G#**   **Am7**   **D7**

__ up! But for now, let's eat _____ up! Be our

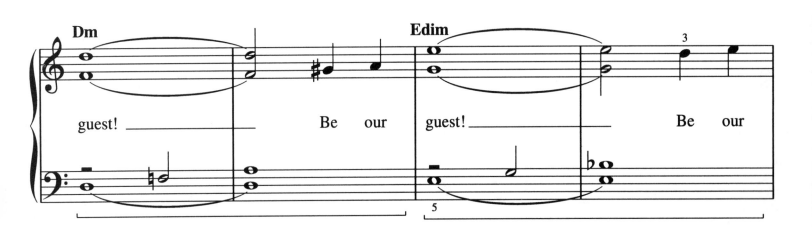

Dm   **Edim**

guest! _____ Be our guest! _____ Be our

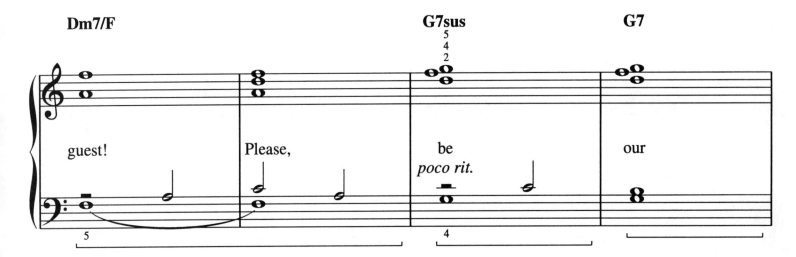

Dm7/F   **G7sus**   **G7**

guest! Please, be our

poco rit.

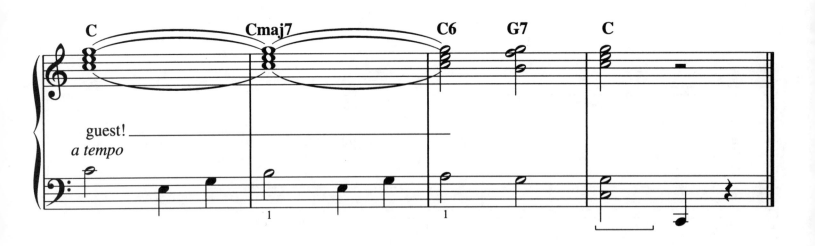

C   **Cmaj7**   **C6**   **G7**   **C**

guest! _____

a tempo

BEAUTY AND THE BEAST

from Walt Disney's BEAUTY AND THE BEAST

Lyrics by HOWARD ASHMAN
Music by ALAN MENKEN

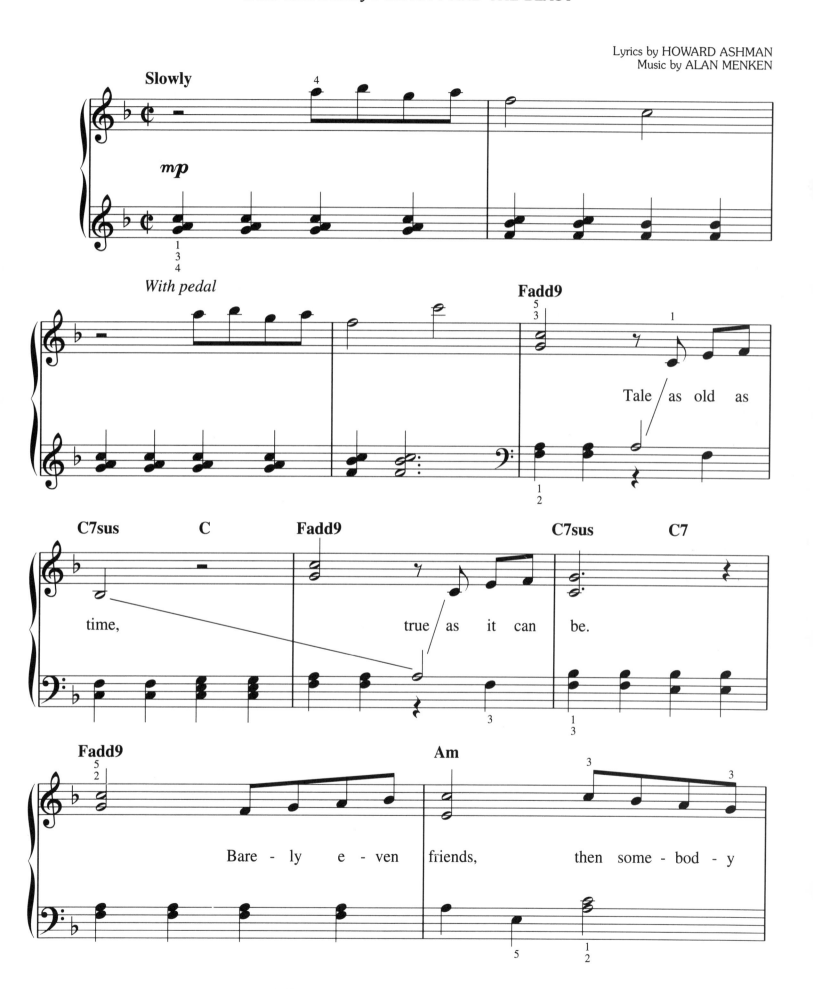

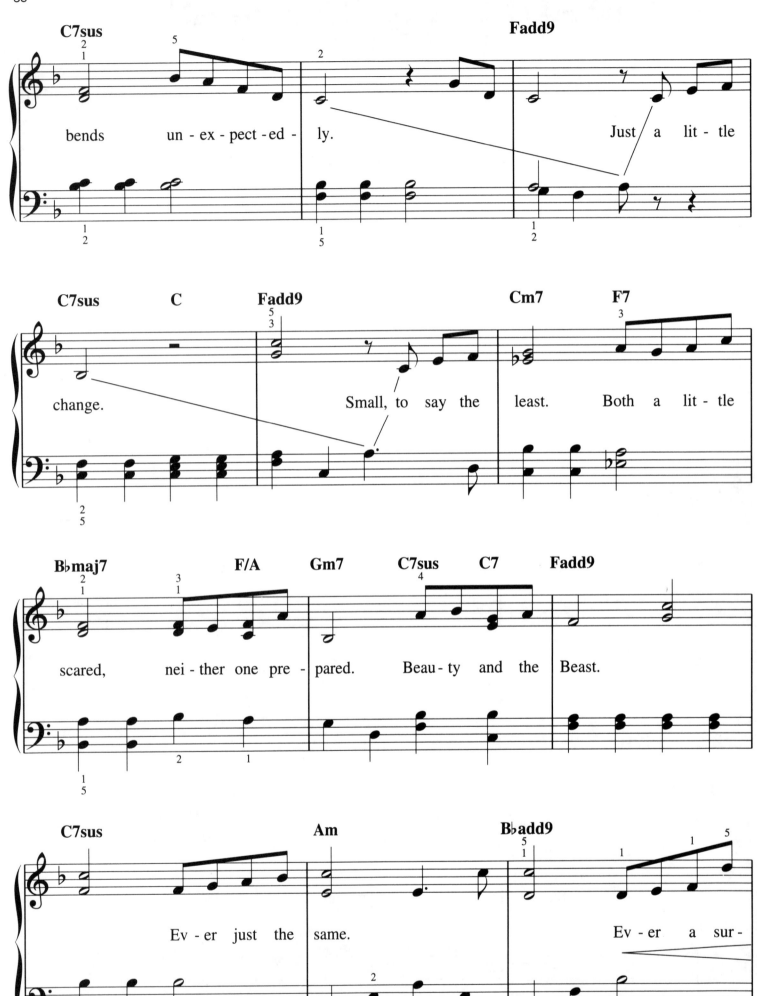

prise.

mf

Ev - er as be - fore, ev - er just as

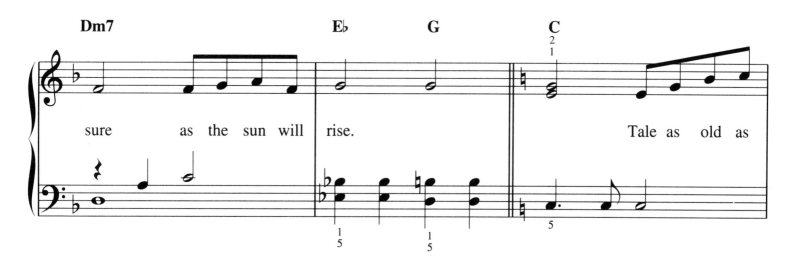

sure as the sun will rise. Tale as old as

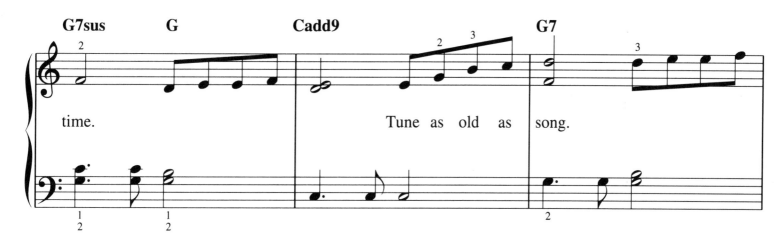

time. Tune as old as song.

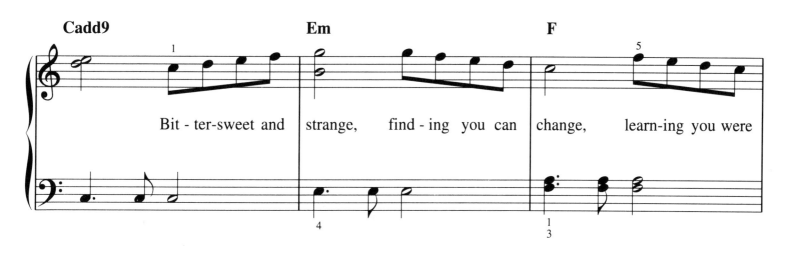

Bit - ter-sweet and strange, find - ing you can change, learn-ing you were

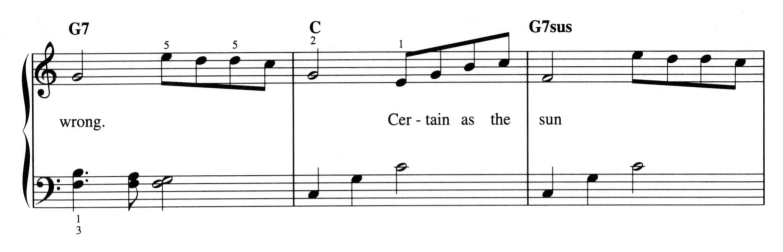

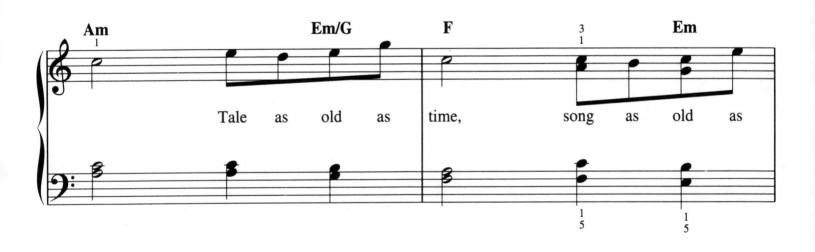

BEST OF FRIENDS
from Walt Disney's THE FOX AND THE HOUND

Words by STAN FIDEL
Music by RICHARD JOHNSTON

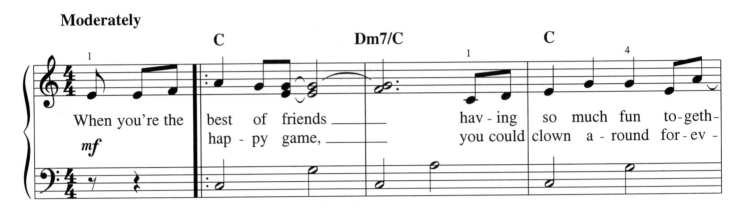

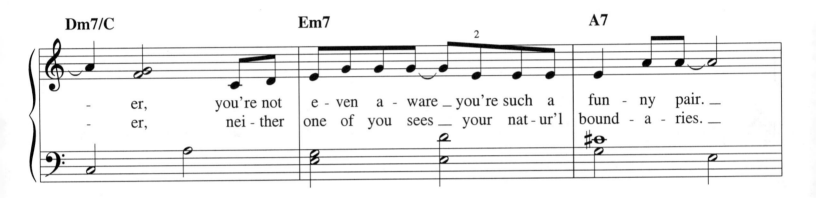

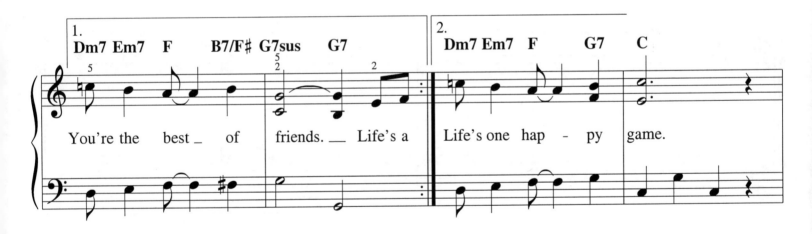

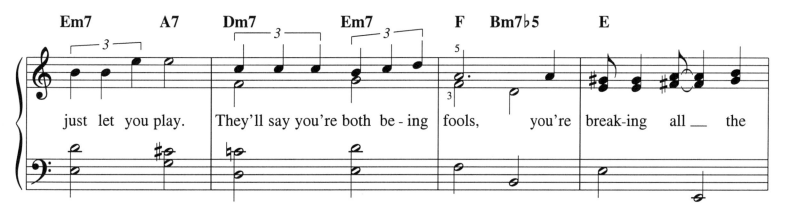

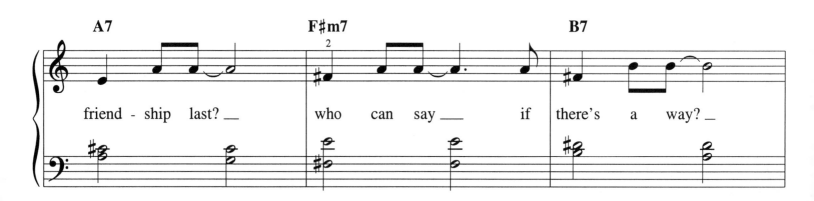

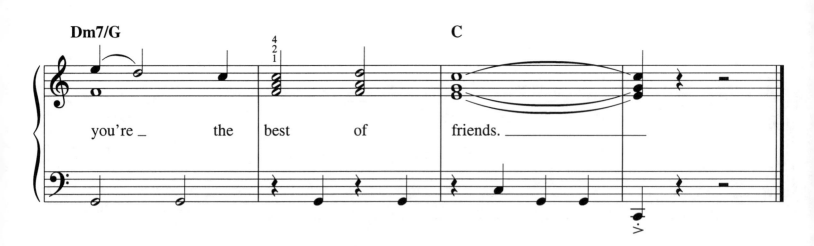

CINDERELLA
from Walt Disney's CINDERELLA

Words and Music by MACK DAVID,
AL HOFFMAN and JERRY LIVINGSTON

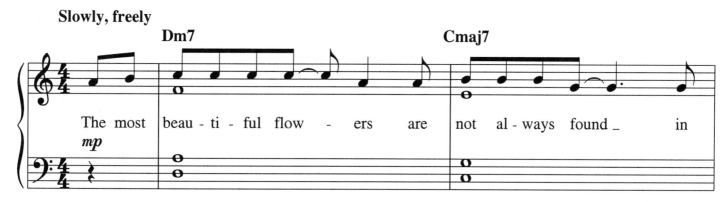

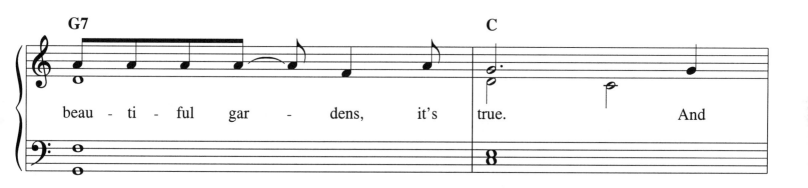

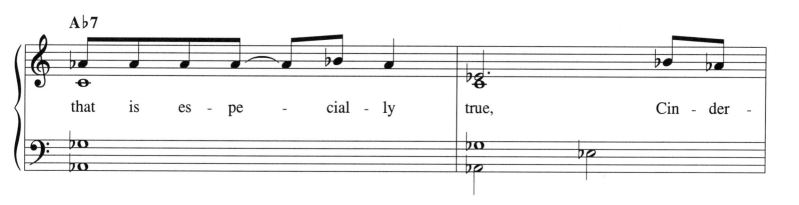

46

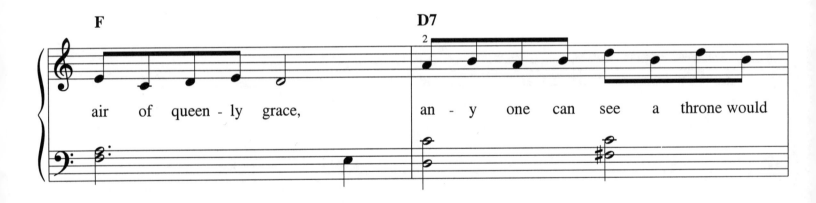

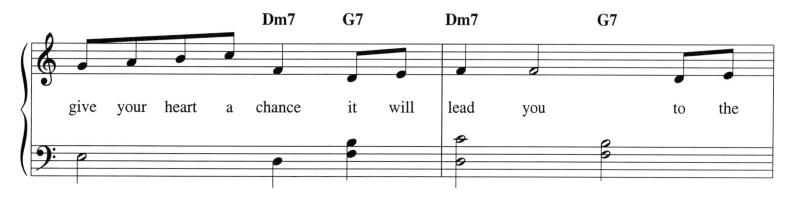

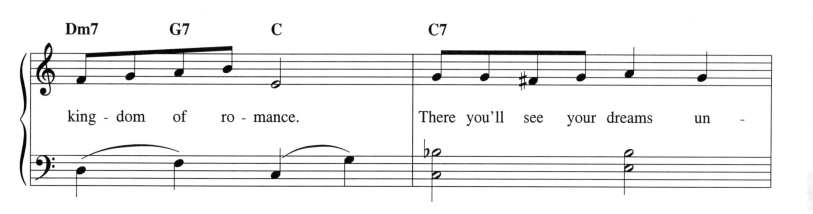

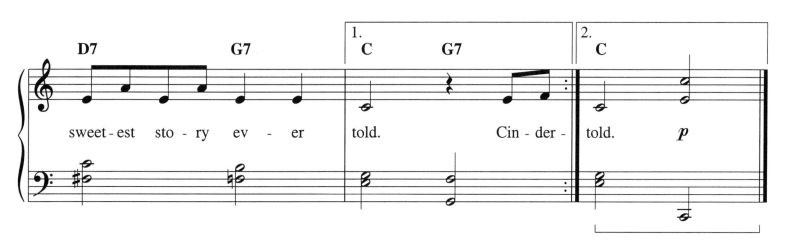

CHIM CHIM CHER-EE
from Walt Disney's MARY POPPINS

Words and Music by RICHARD M. SHERMAN
and ROBERT B. SHERMAN

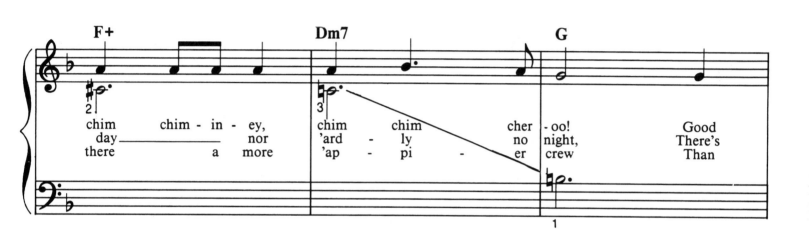
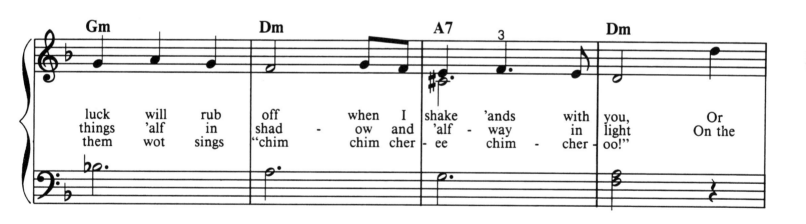
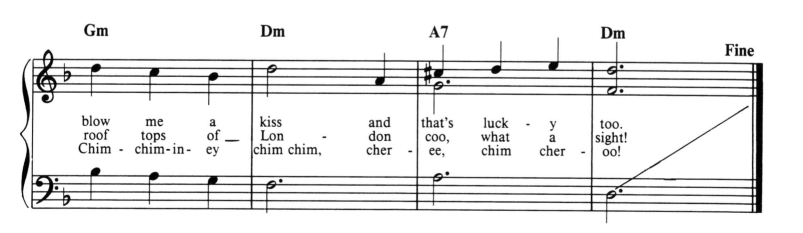

THE COURT OF MIRACLES

from Walt Disney's THE HUNCHBACK OF NOTRE DAME

Music by ALAN MENKEN
Lyrics by STEPHEN SCHWARTZ

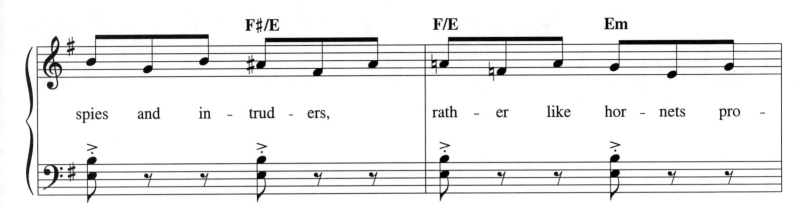

spies and in - trud - ers, rath - er like hor - nets pro -

tect - ing their hive. Here in the Court ____ of

Mir - a - cles where it's a mir - a - cle if you get

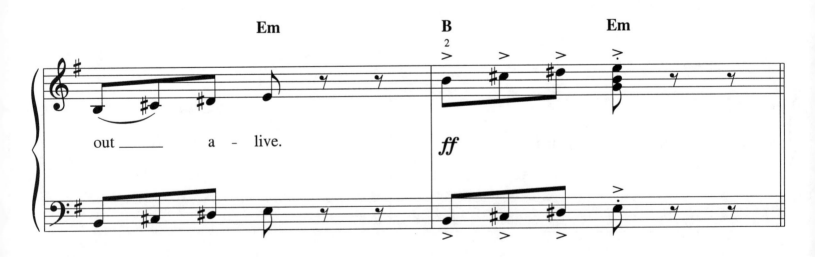

out ____ a - live. *ff*

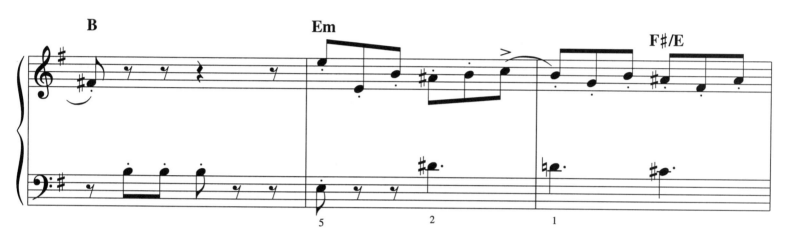

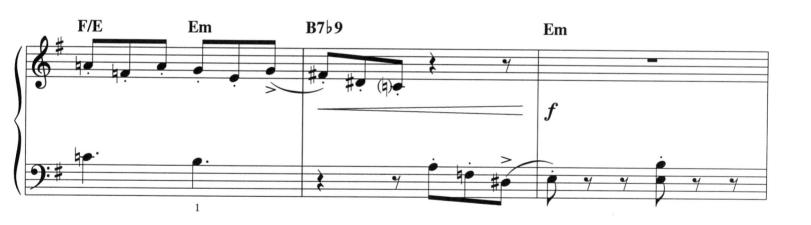

54

CRUELLA DE VIL
from Walt Disney's 101 DALMATIANS

Words and Music by
MEL LEVEN

curl of her lips, ___ the ice in her stare; ___ All

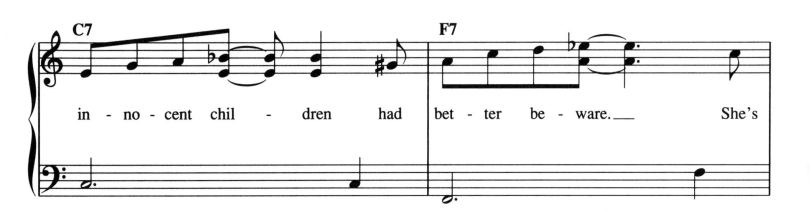

in - no - cent chil - dren had bet - ter be - ware. ___ She's

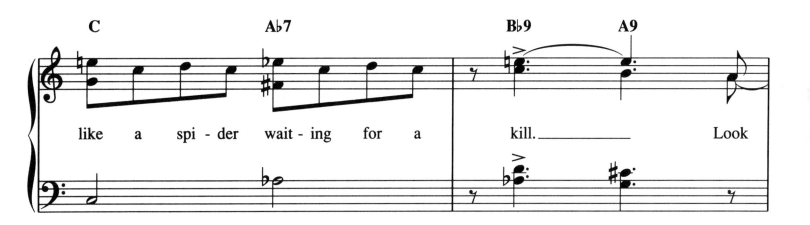

like a spi - der wait - ing for a kill. _____ Look

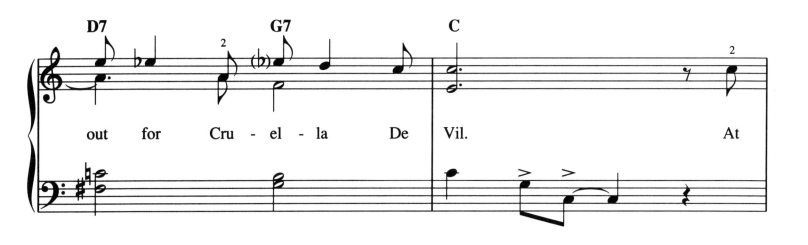

out for Cru - el - la De Vil. At

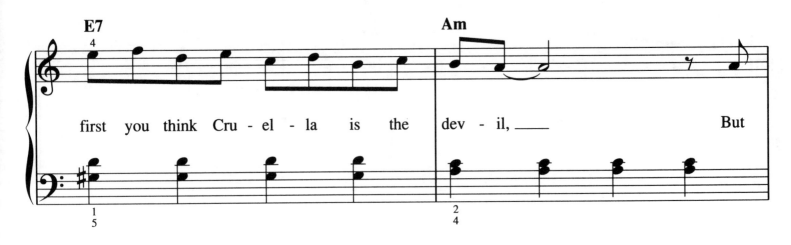

first you think Cru - el - la is the dev - il, _____ But

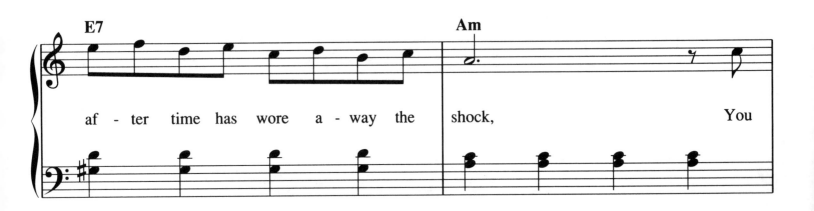

af - ter time has wore a - way the shock, You

come to re - al - ize you've seen her kind of eyes

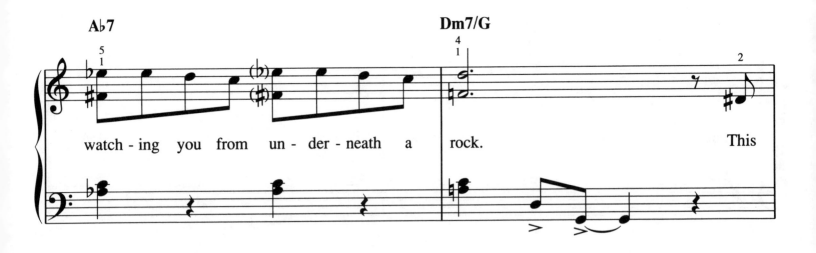

watch - ing you from un - der - neath a rock. This

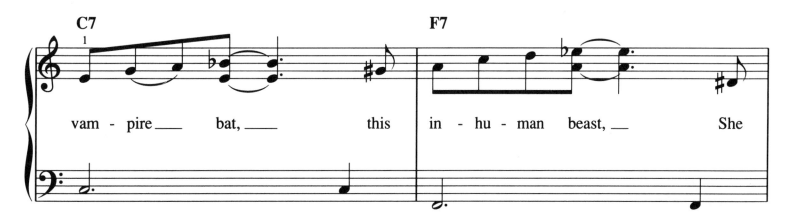

vam - pire ___ bat, ___ this in - hu - man beast, ___ She

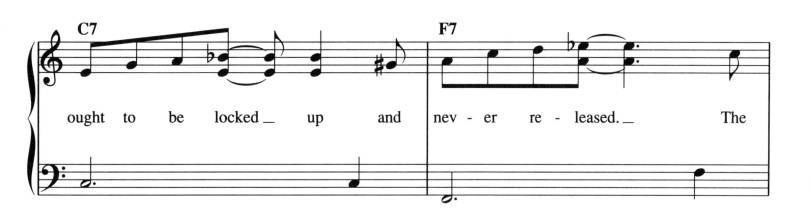

ought to be locked ___ up and nev - er re - leased. ___ The

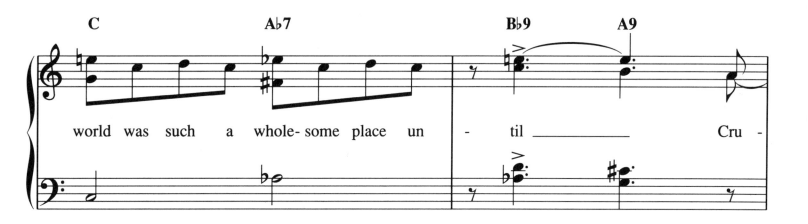

world was such a whole- some place un - til _____ Cru -

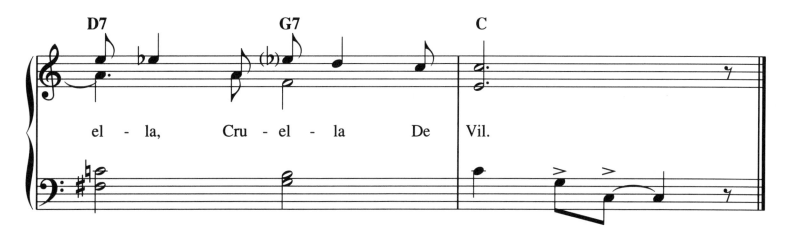

el - la, Cru - el - la De Vil.

FOLLOWING THE LEADER
from Walt Disney's PETER PAN

Words by TED SEARS and WINSTON HIBLER
Music by OLIVER WALLACE

Gaily (in 2; ♩. = 1 beat)

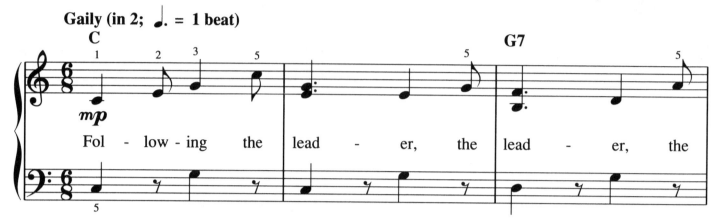

Fol - low - ing the lead - er, the lead - er, the

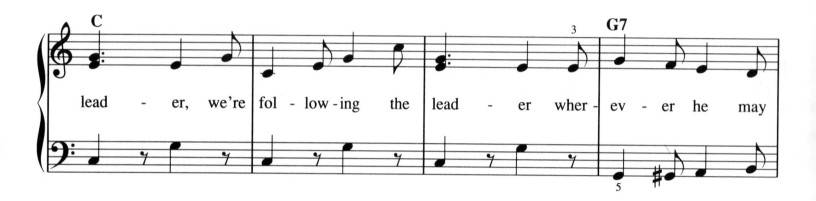

lead - er, we're fol - low - ing the lead - er wher - ev - er he may

go. _____ We won't be home till morn - ing, till morn - ing, till

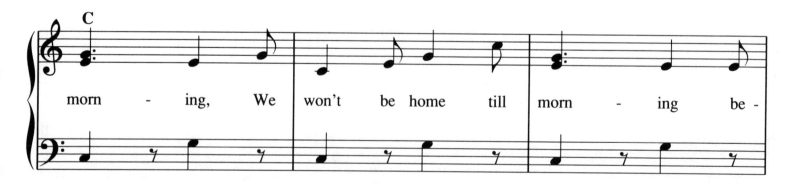

morn - ing, We won't be home till morn - ing be -

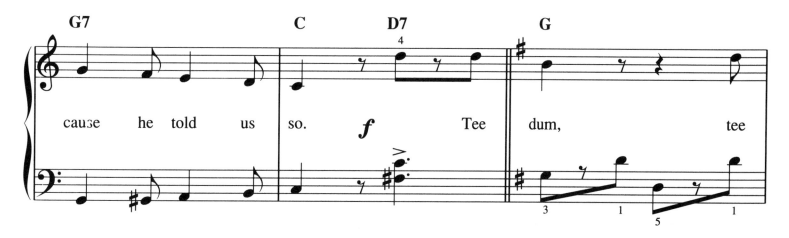

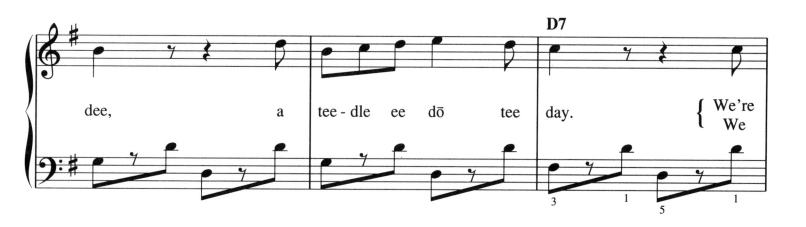

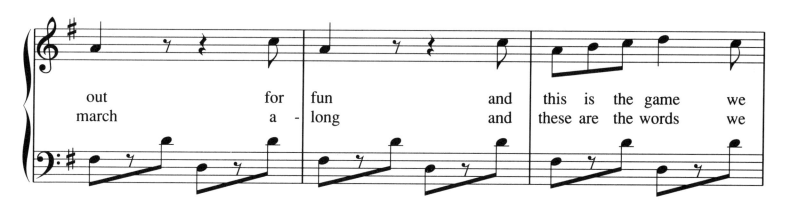

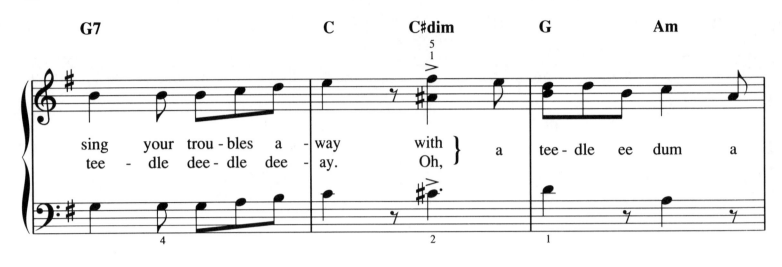

sing your trou - bles a - way with
tee - dle dee-dle dee - ay. Oh, } a tee - dle ee dum a

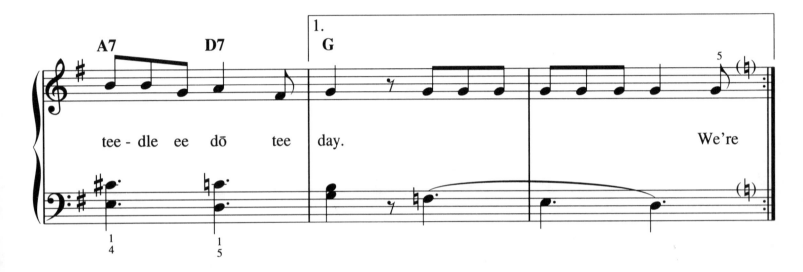

tee - dle ee dō tee day. We're

day. Oh, a tee - dle ee dum, a

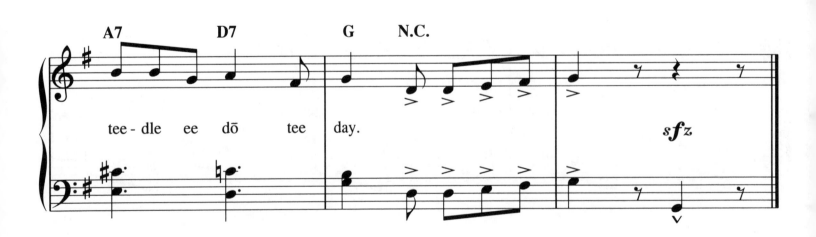

tee - dle ee dō tee day. *sfz*

A GUY LIKE YOU

from Walt Disney's THE HUNCHBACK OF NOTRE DAME

Music by ALAN MENKEN
Lyrics by STEPHEN SCHWARTZ

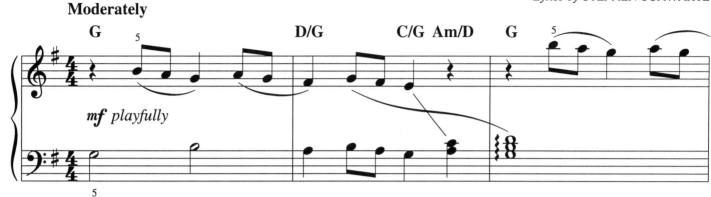

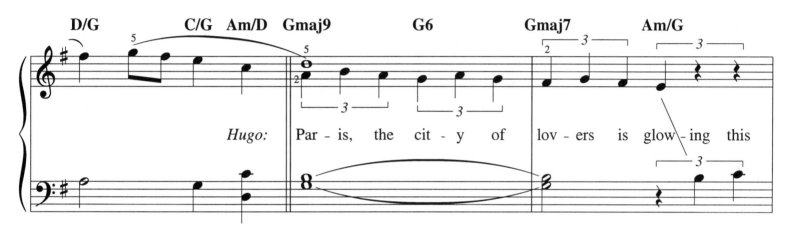

Hugo: Par - is, the cit - y of lov - ers is glow - ing this

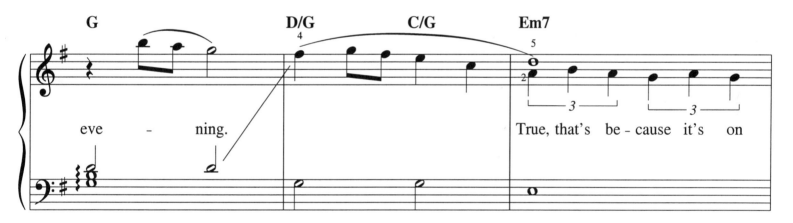

eve - ning. True, that's be - cause it's on

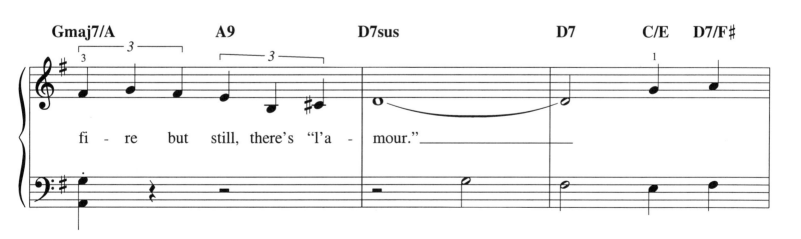

fi - re but still, there's "l'a - mour."

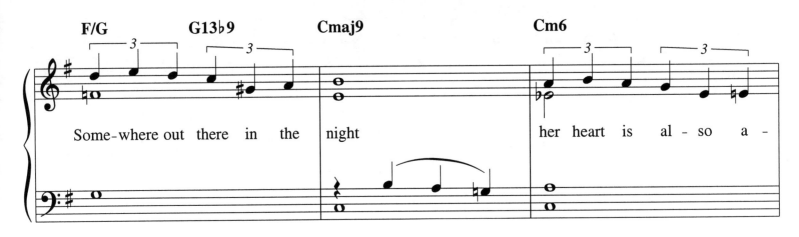

Some-where out there in the night her heart is al - so a -

light, and I know the guy she just might be burn - ing

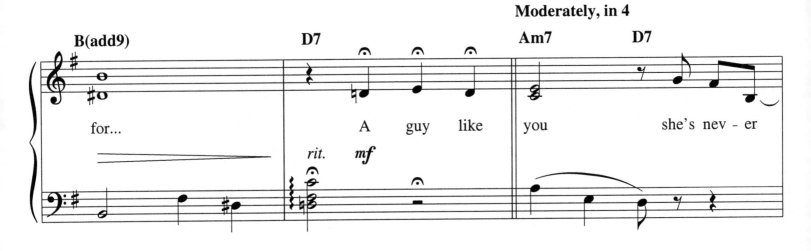

Moderately, in 4

for... *rit.* *mf* A guy like you she's nev - er

known, kid. A guy like you a girl does not meet ev - 'ry

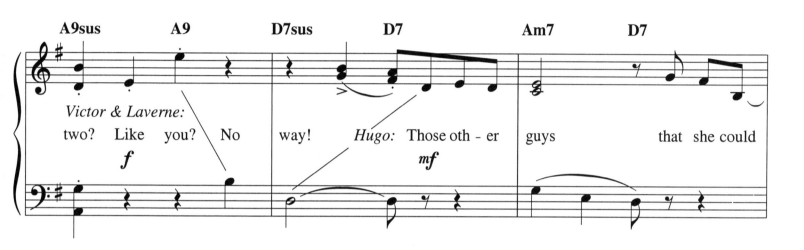

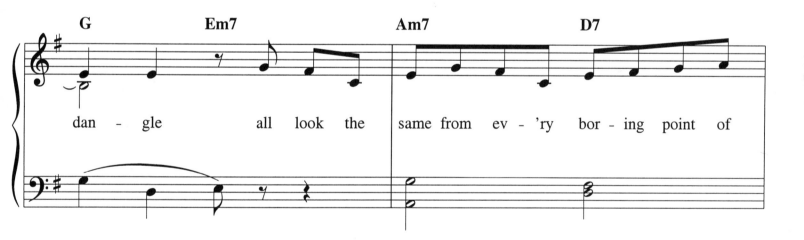

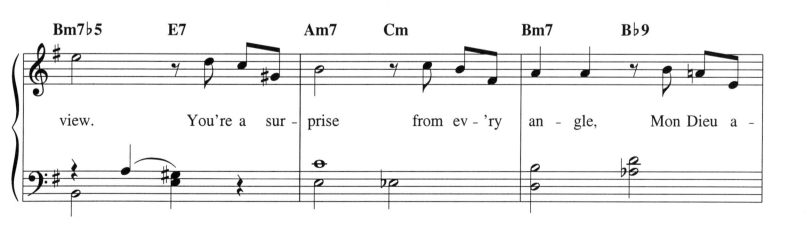

bove, she's got-ta love a guy like you. *Victor:* A guy like

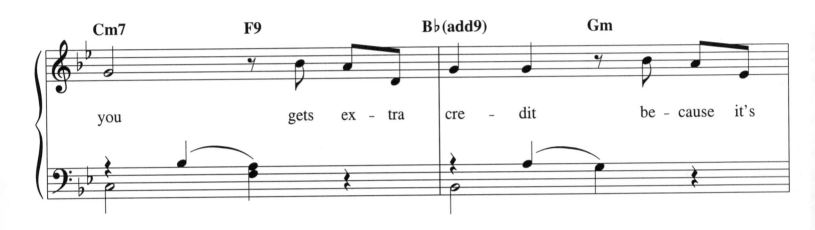

you gets ex-tra cre - dit be-cause it's

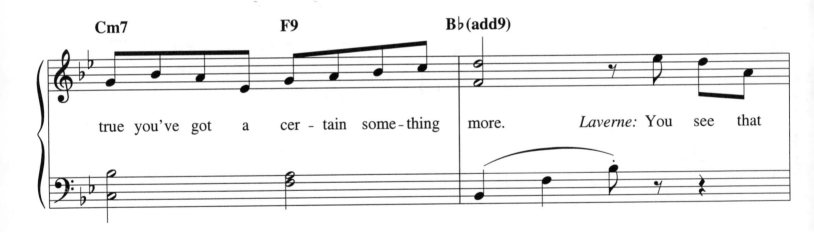

true you've got a cer-tain some-thing more. *Laverne:* You see that

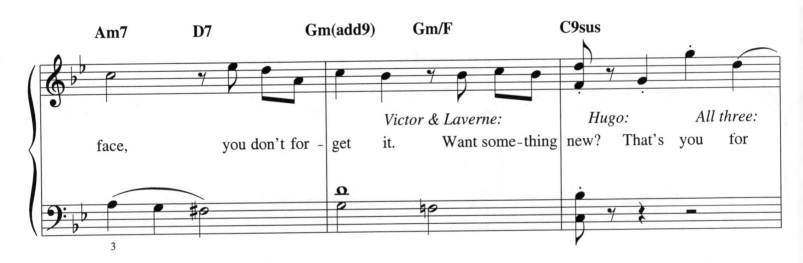

face, you don't for - get it. Want some-thing new? That's you for

Victor & Laverne: *Hugo:* *All three:*

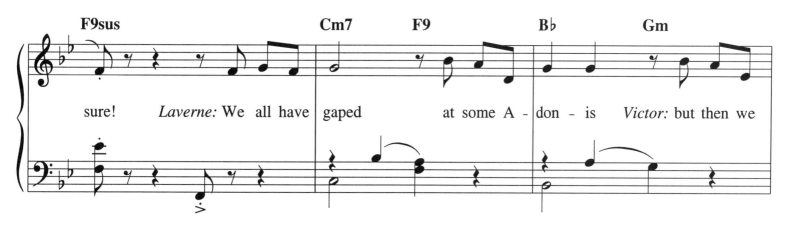

sure! *Laverne:* We all have gaped at some A - don - is *Victor:* but then we

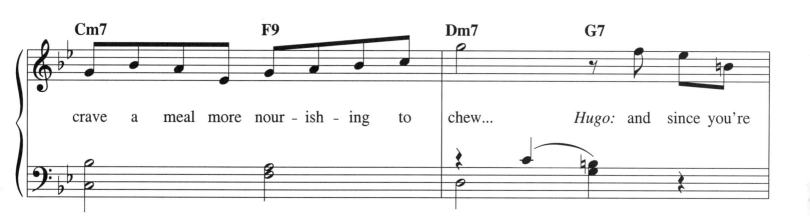

crave a meal more nour - ish - ing to chew... *Hugo:* and since you're

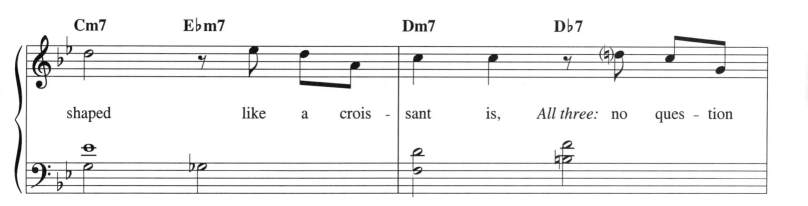

shaped like a crois - sant is, *All three:* no ques - tion

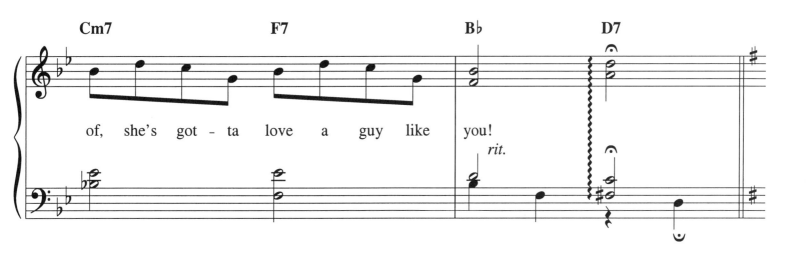

of, she's got - ta love a guy like you!

rit.

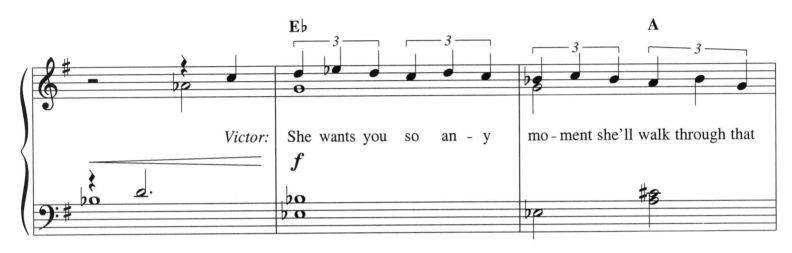

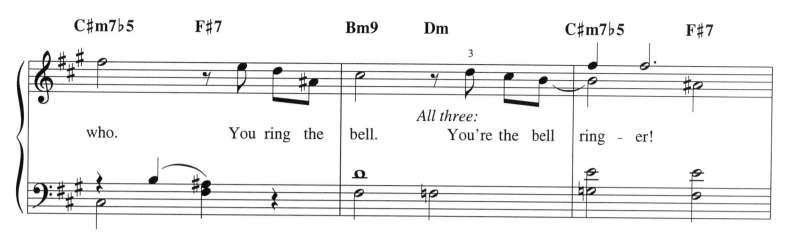

who.   You ring the   bell.   *All three:*   You're the bell   ring - er!

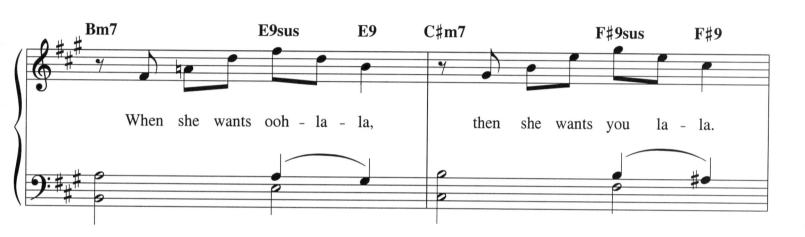

When she wants ooh - la - la,   then   she wants you   la - la.

She will dis-cov-er, guy,   you're one heck-uv - a guy.   Who would-n't love   a

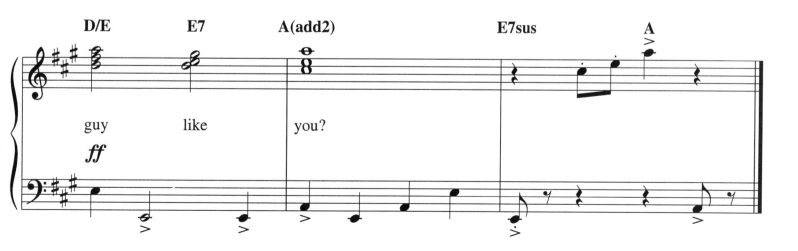

guy   like   you?

ff

GO THE DISTANCE

from Walt Disney Pictures' HERCULES

Music by ALAN MENKEN
Lyrics by DAVID ZIPPEL

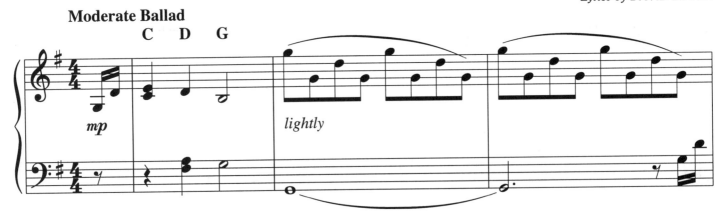

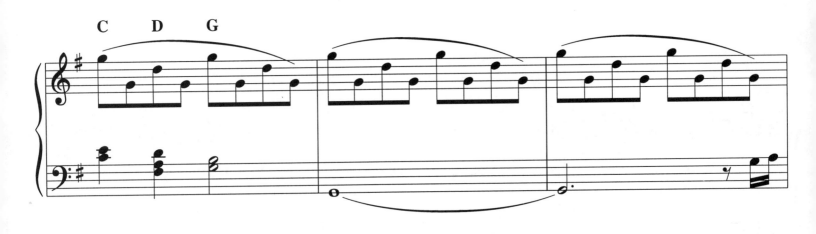

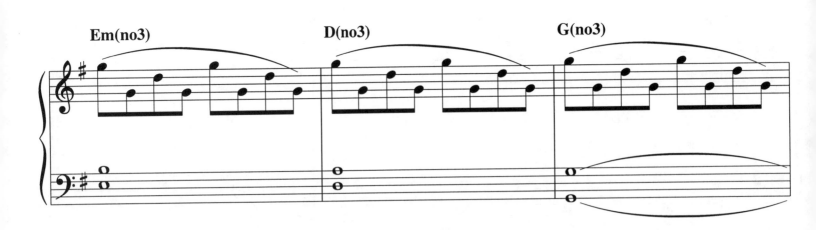

Young Hercules: I have of - ten dreamed of a far - off place where a

great warm wel-come will be wait - ing for me. Where the crowds will cheer when they

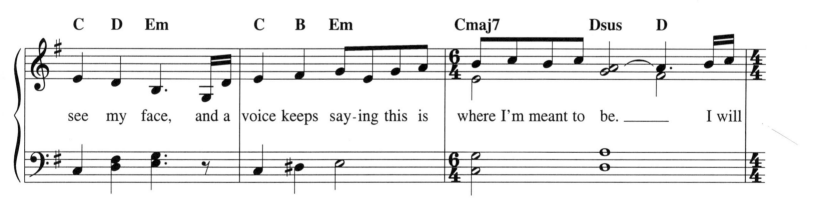

see my face, and a voice keeps say-ing this is where I'm meant to be. _____ I will

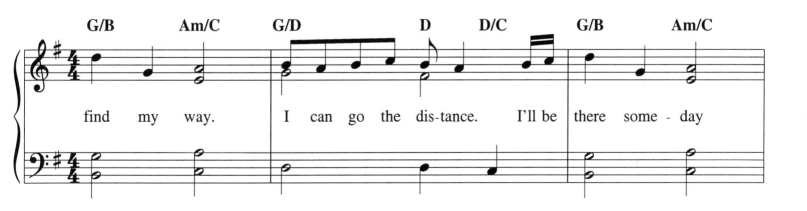

find my way. I can go the dis-tance. I'll be there some - day

72

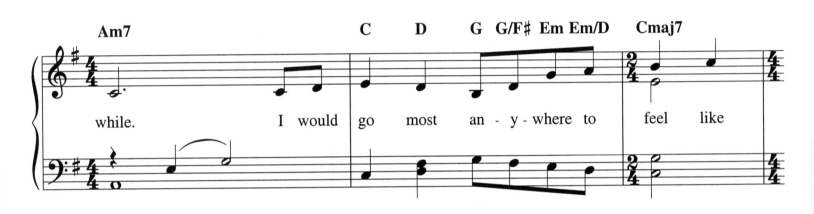

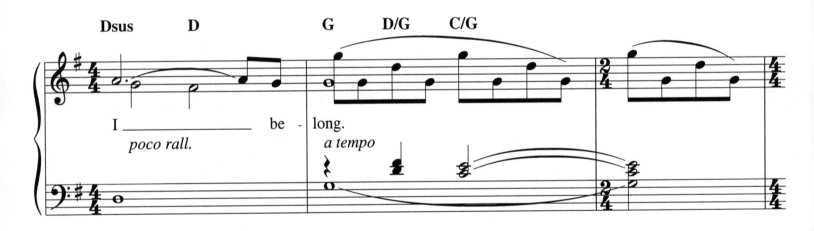

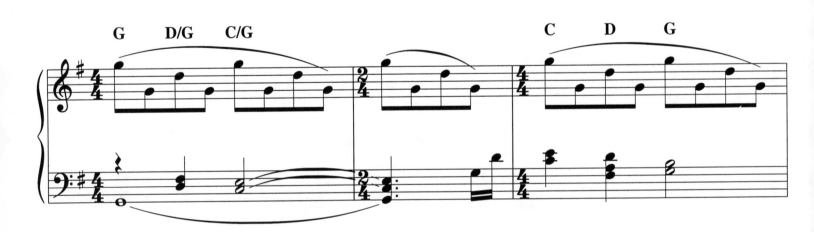

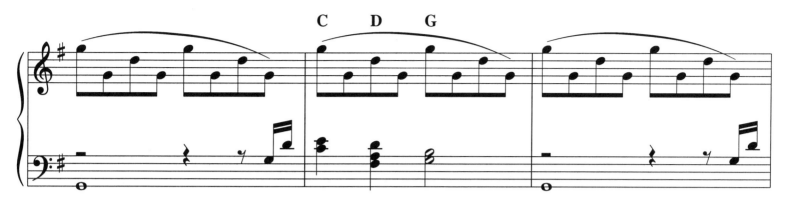

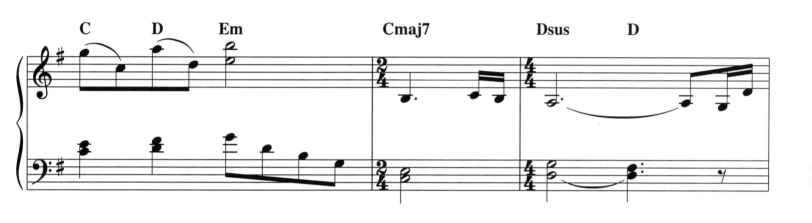

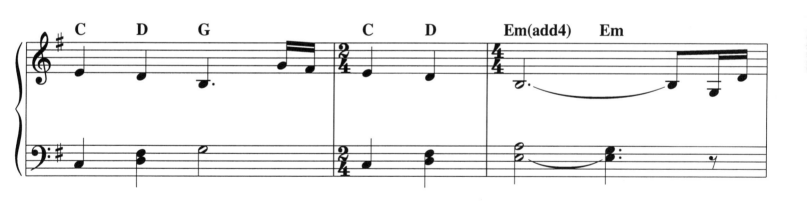

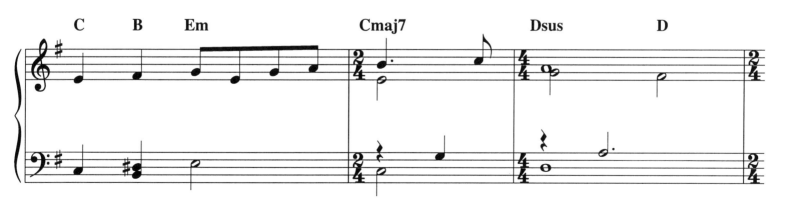

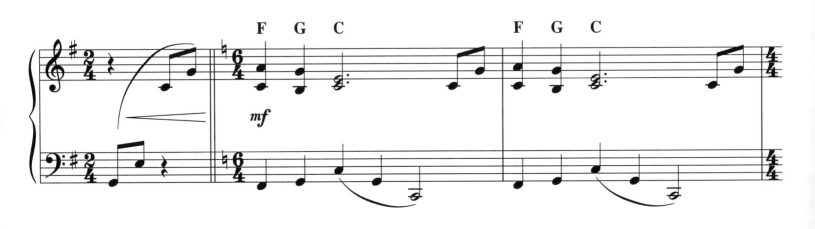

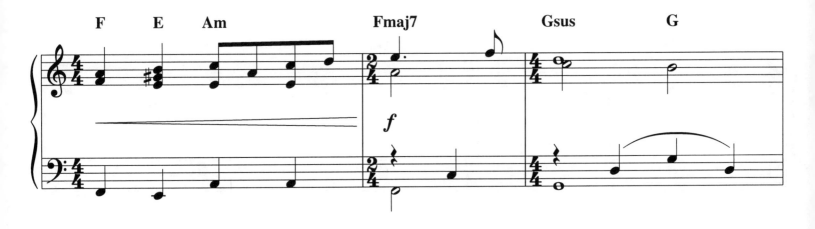

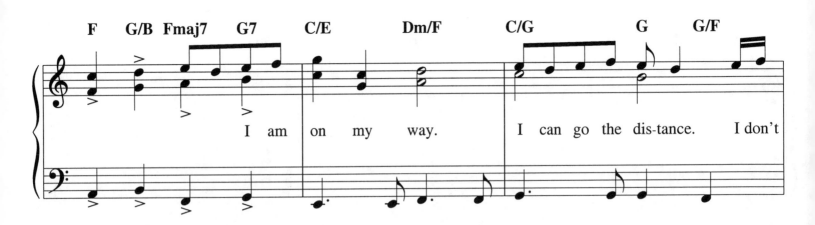

I am on my way. I can go the dis-tance. I don't

care how far, some-how I'll be strong. I know ev - 'ry mile will be

worth my while. I would go most an - y - where to

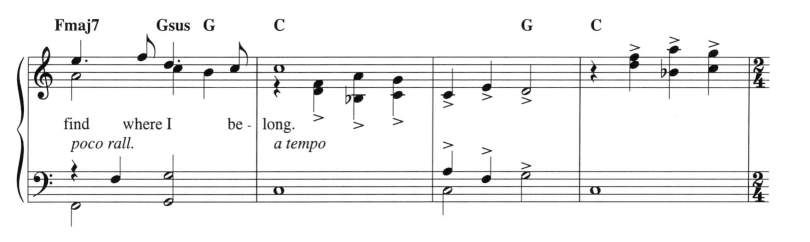

find where I be - long.
poco rall. *a tempo*

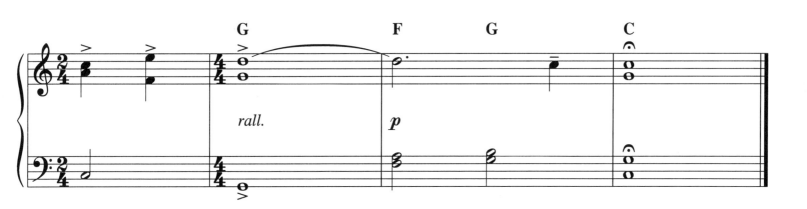

rall. *p*

HAKUNA MATATA

from Walt Disney Pictures' THE LION KING

Music by ELTON JOHN
Lyrics by TIM RICE

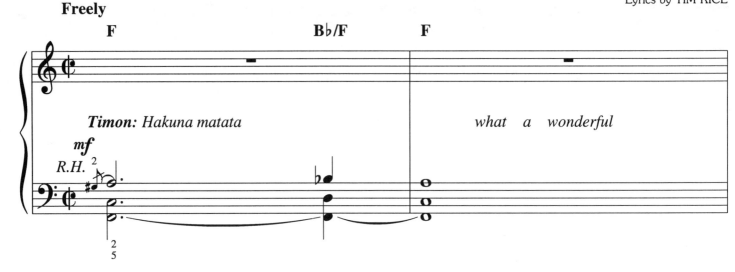

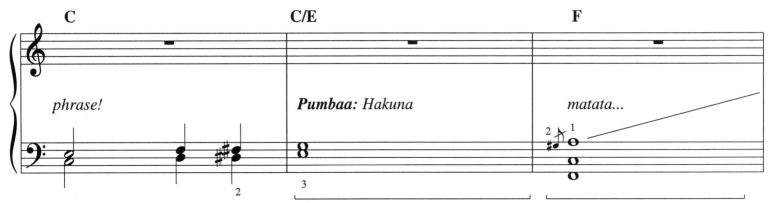

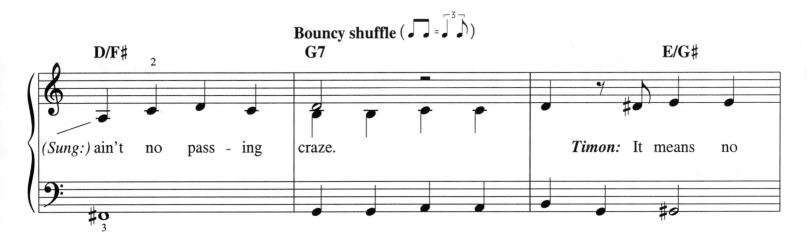

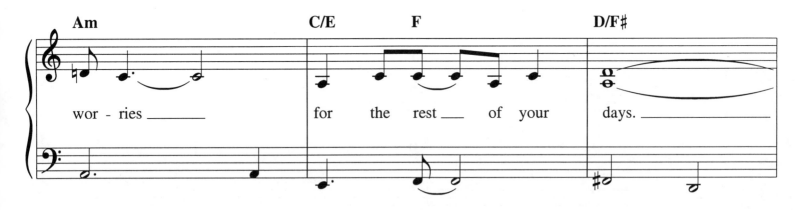

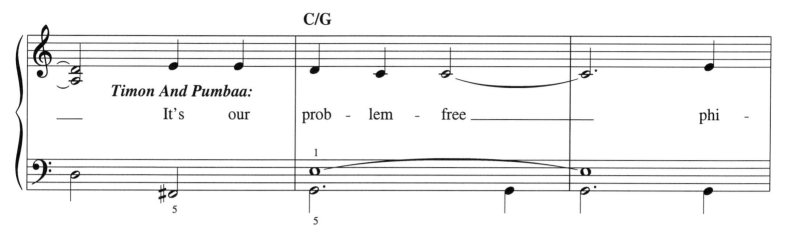

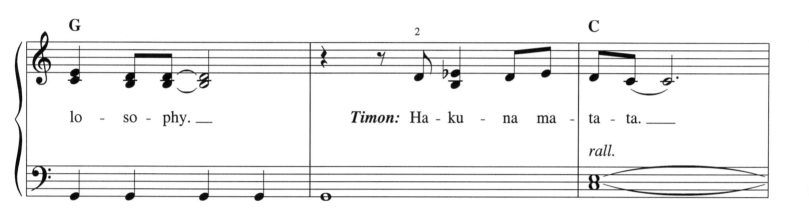

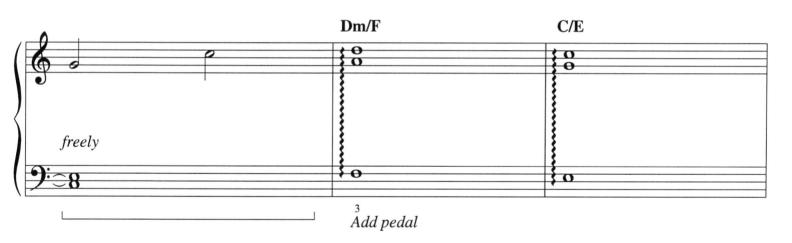

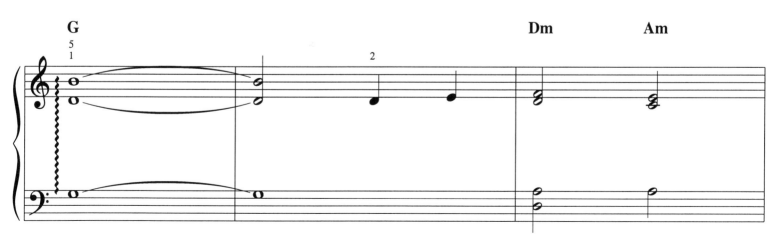

G **N.C.** **Bb** **F**

Timon: When he was a young wart -

f

No pedal

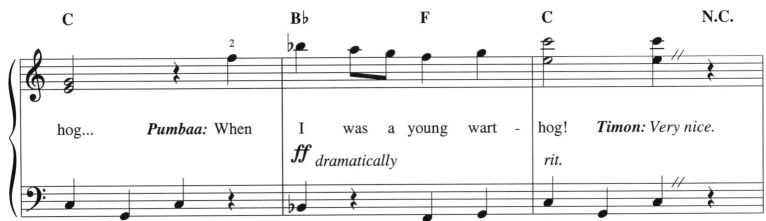

C **Bb** **F** **C** **N.C.**

hog... *Pumbaa:* When I was a young wart - hog! *Timon: Very nice.*

ff dramatically *rit.*

Eb **F**

Pumbaa: *Timon:*

Thanks. He found his a - ro - ma lacked a cer - tain ap - peal.___ He could

mf *quickly*

C **G** **Bb**

Pumbaa:

clear the sa - van - nah af - ter ev - 'ry meal!___ I'm a sen - si - tive soul,

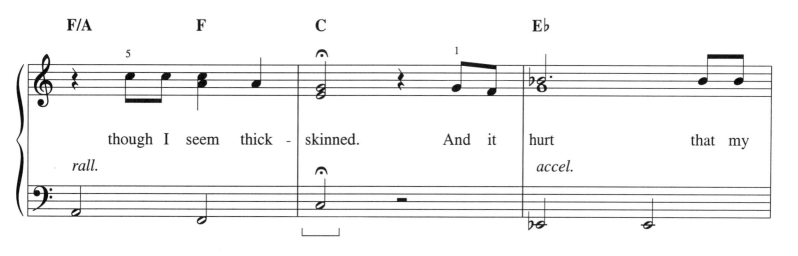

though I seem thick - skinned. And it hurt that my
rall. *accel.*

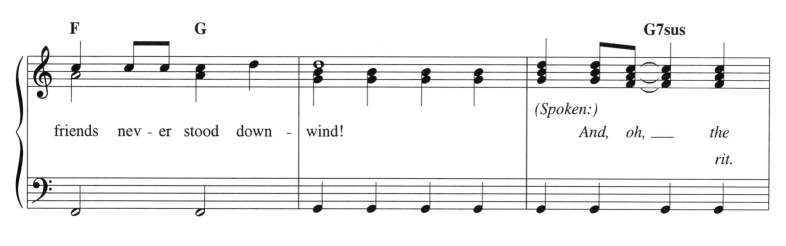

friends nev - er stood down - wind!
(Spoken:)
And, oh, ___ the
rit.

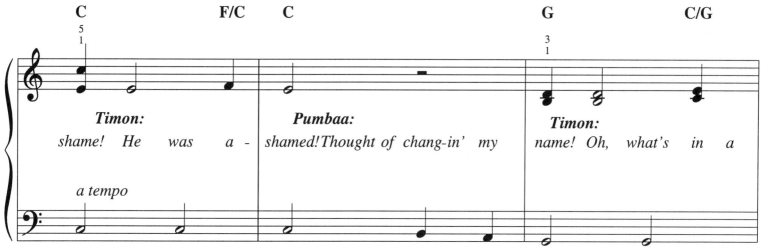

Timon:
shame! He was a -
a tempo

Pumbaa:
shamed! Thought of chang-in' my

Timon:
name! Oh, what's in a

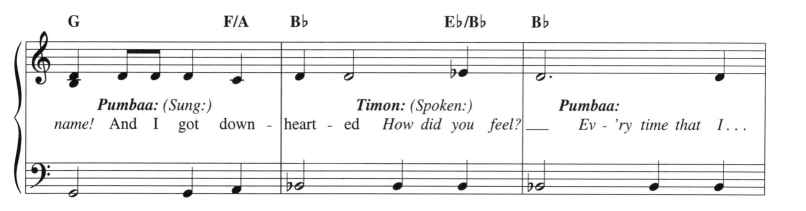

Pumbaa: *(Sung:)*
name! And I got down -

Timon: *(Spoken:)*
heart - ed *How did you feel?* ___

Pumbaa:
Ev - 'ry time that I . . .

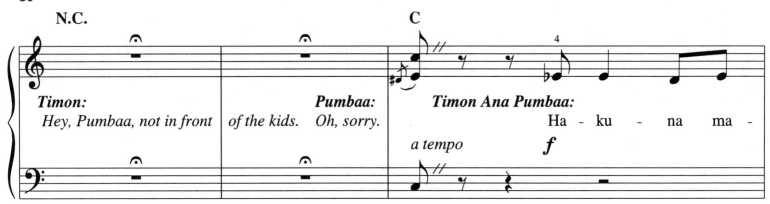

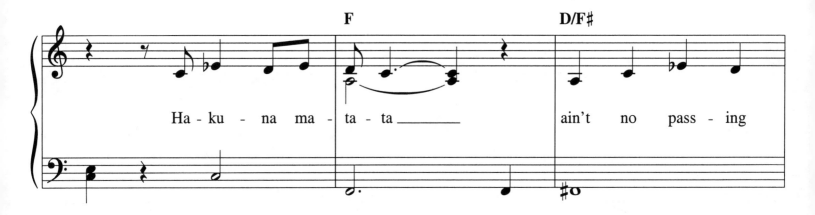

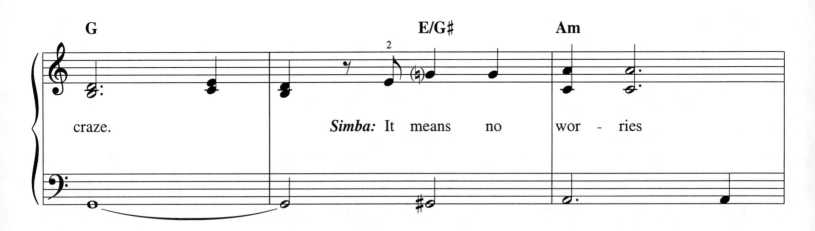

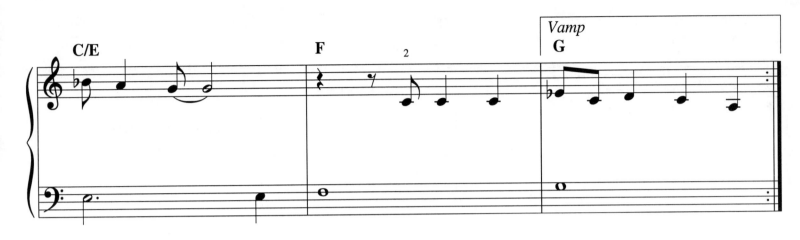

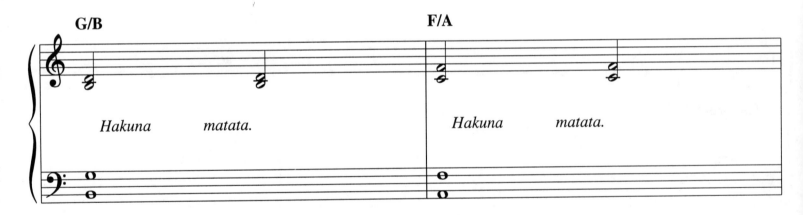

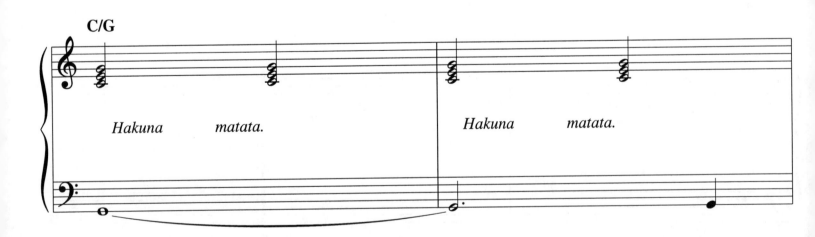

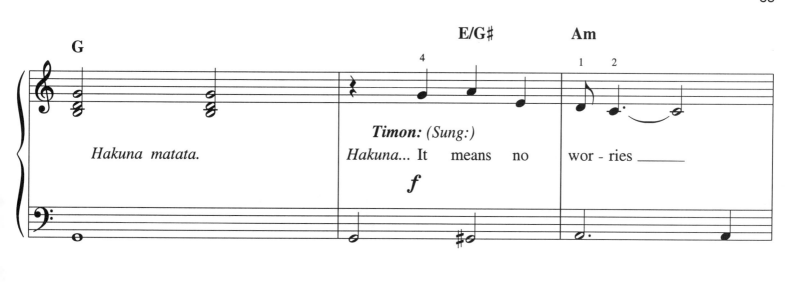

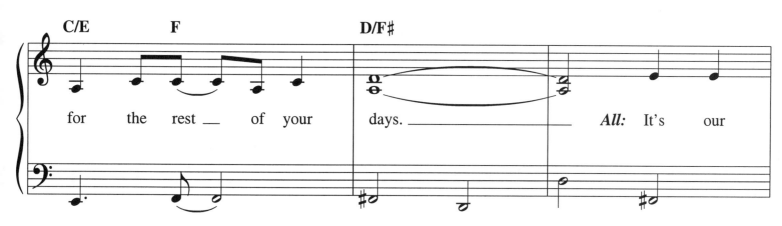

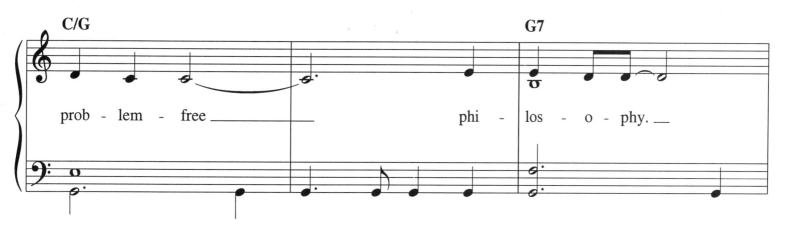

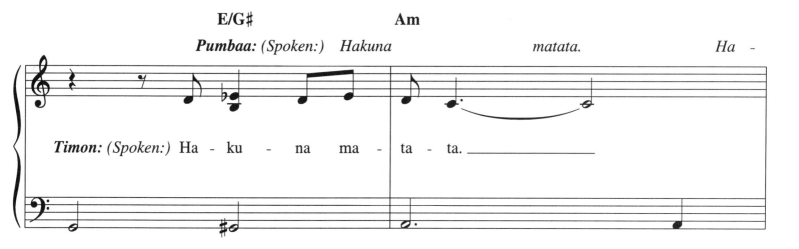

HIGITUS FIGITUS
from Walt Disney's THE SWORD IN THE STONE

Words and Music by RICHARD M. SHERMAN
and ROBERT B. SHERMAN

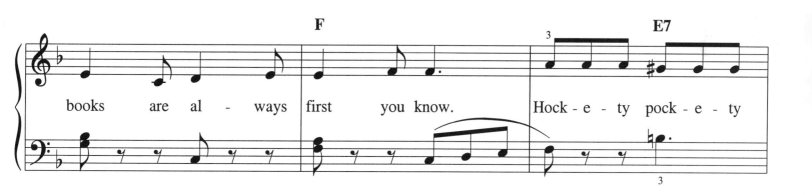

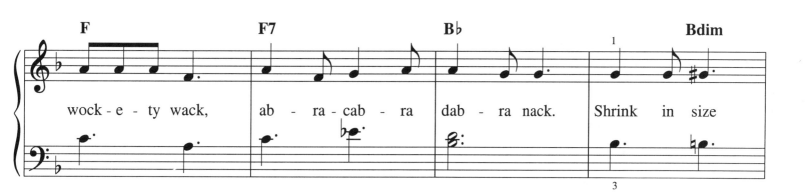

ver - y small, we've got to save e - nough room for all.

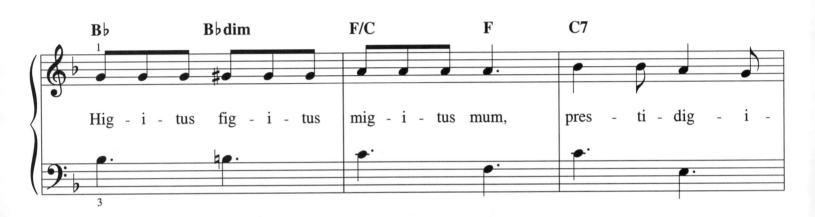

Hig - i - tus fig - i - tus mig - i - tus mum, pres - ti - dig - i -

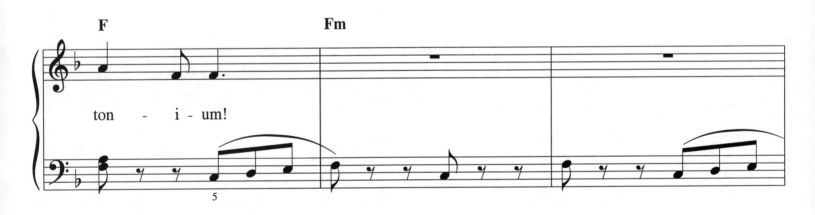

ton - i - um!

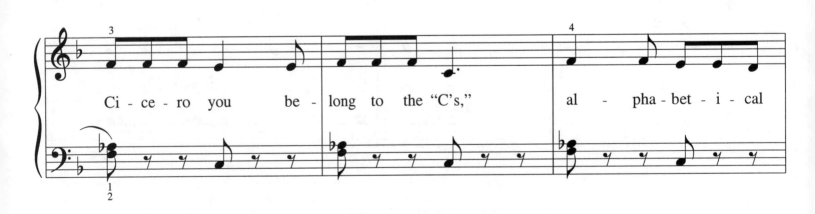

Ci - ce - ro you be - long to the "C's," al - pha - bet - i - cal

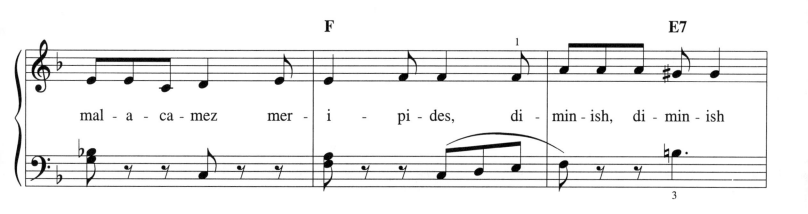

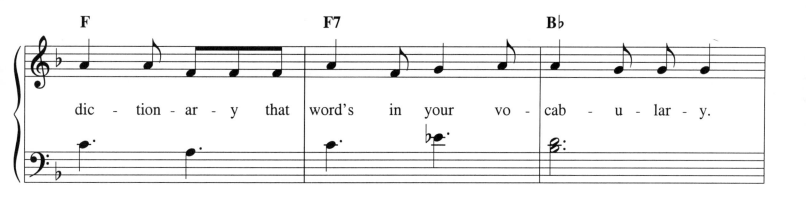

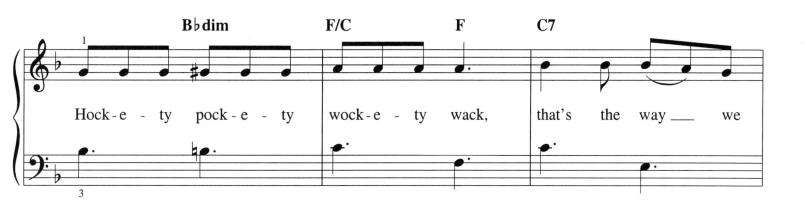

F   B♭   B♭dim   F/C   F

have to pack. Hig - i - tus fig - i - tus mig - i - tus mum,

C7   F   Fm

pres - ti - dig - i - ton - i - um.

Hig - i - tus fig - i - tus zoom - a - ca - zam,

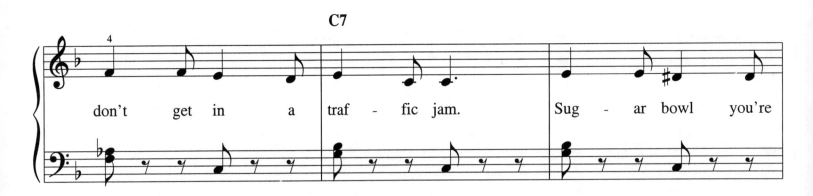

C7

don't get in a traf - fic jam. Sug - ar bowl you're

get - ting rough, the poor old tea set's cracked e - nough.

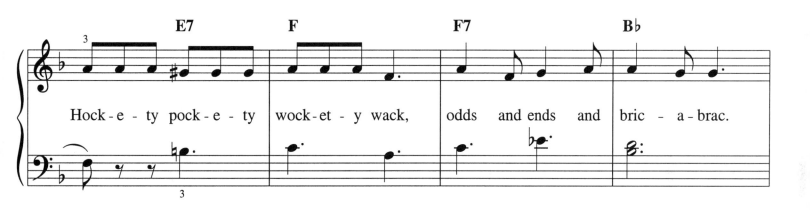

Hock - e - ty pock - e - ty wock - et - y wack, odds and ends and bric - a - brac.

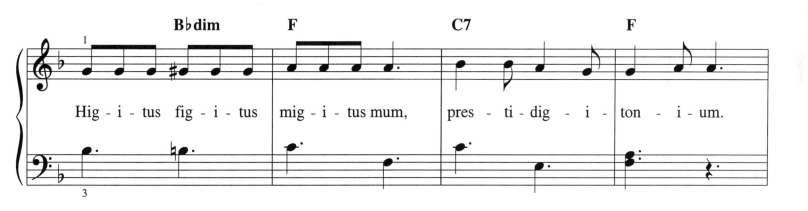

Hig - i - tus fig - i - tus mig - i - tus mum, pres - ti - dig - i - ton - i - um.

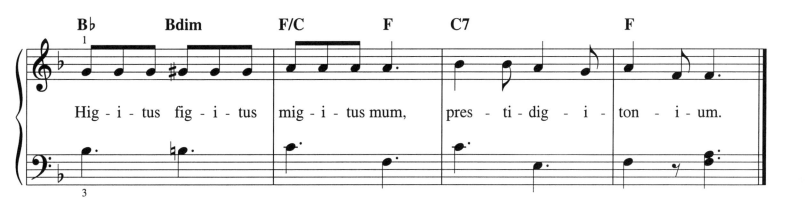

Hig - i - tus fig - i - tus mig - i - tus mum, pres - ti - dig - i - ton - i - um.

HONOR TO US ALL

from Walt Disney Pictures' MULAN

Music by MATTHEW WILDER
Lyrics by DAVID ZIPPEL

Very quickly, in 2

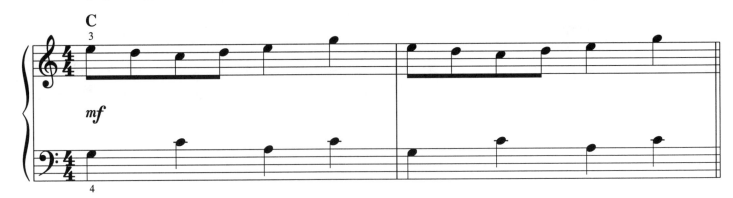

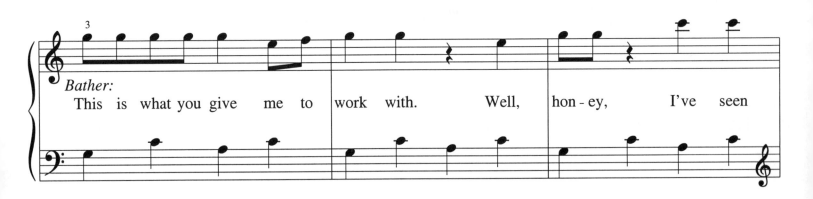

Bather:
This is what you give me to work with. Well, hon - ey, I've seen

worse.   We're going to turn this sow's ear

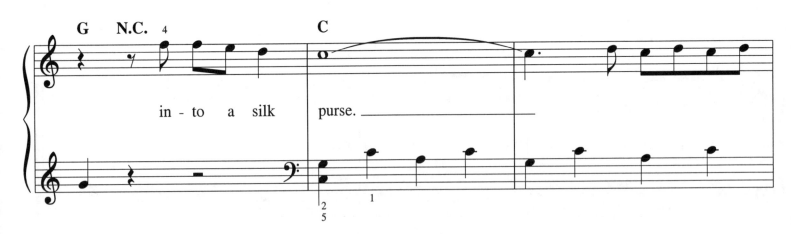

in - to a silk purse. _____

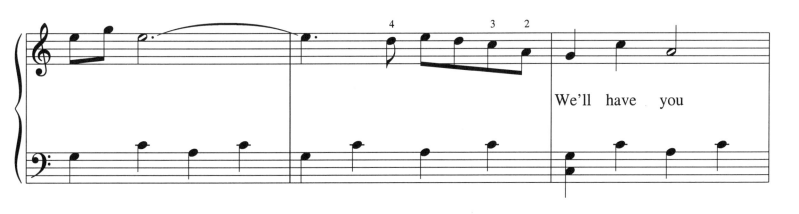

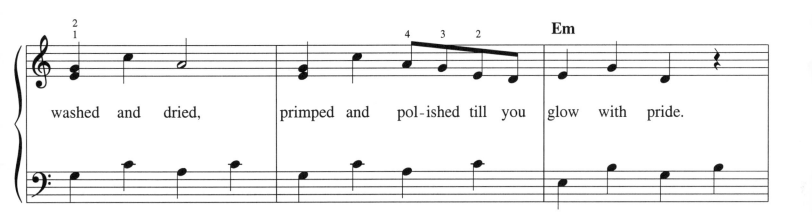

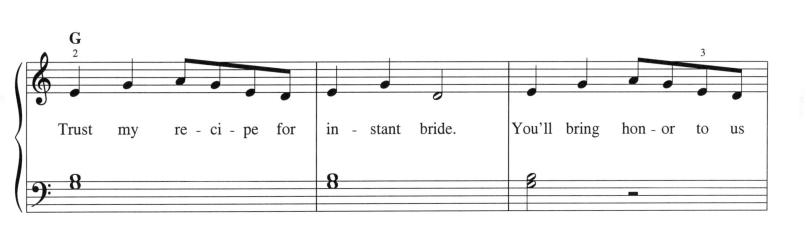

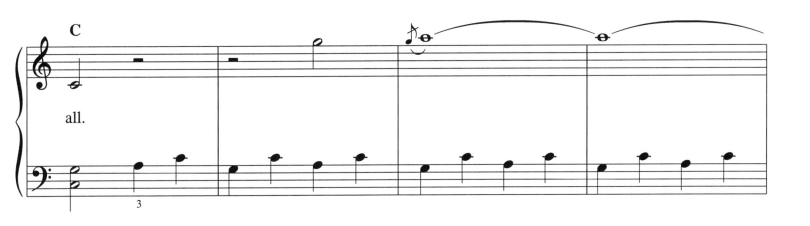

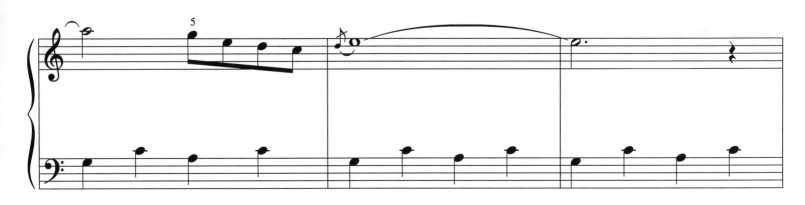

Hairdresser 1:
Wait and see.

When we're through

Hairdresser 2:
boys will glad - ly go to

war for you.

Hairdresser 1:
With good for - tune and a

Hairdresser 2:
great hair - do

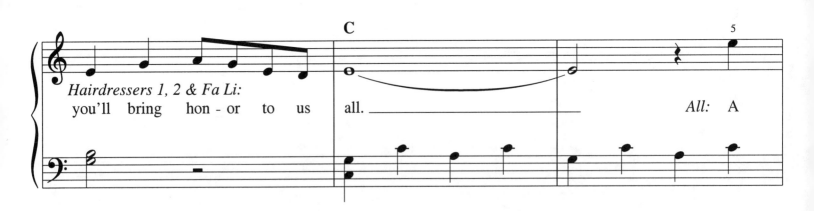

Hairdressers 1, 2 & Fa Li:
you'll bring hon - or to us all. _____

All: A

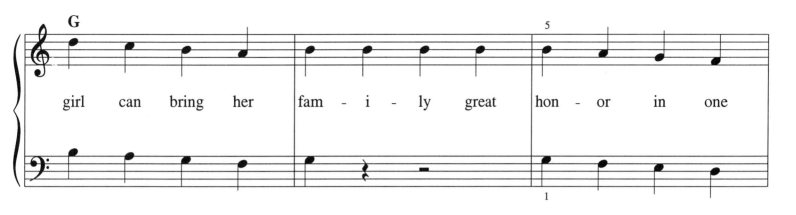

girl can bring her fam - i - ly great hon - or in one

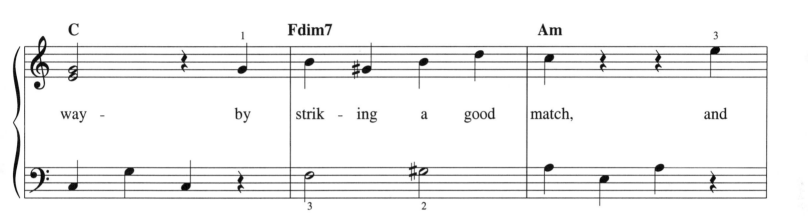

way - by strik - ing a good match, and

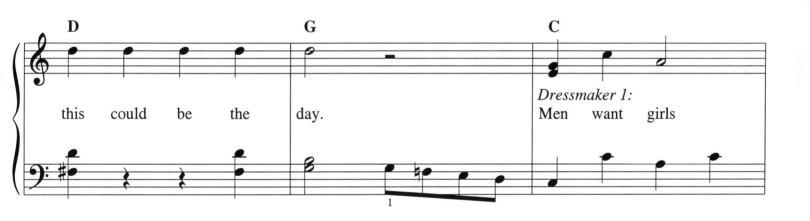

this could be the day.

Dressmaker 1:
Men want girls

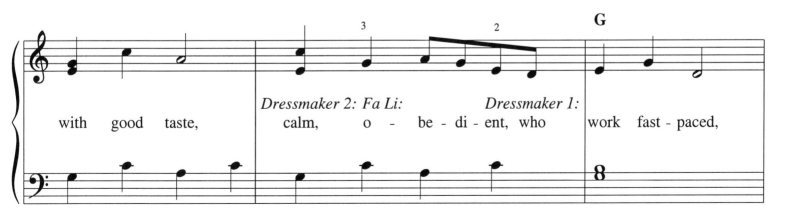

with good taste,

Dressmaker 2: Fa Li: *Dressmaker 1:*
calm, o - be - di - ent, who work fast - paced,

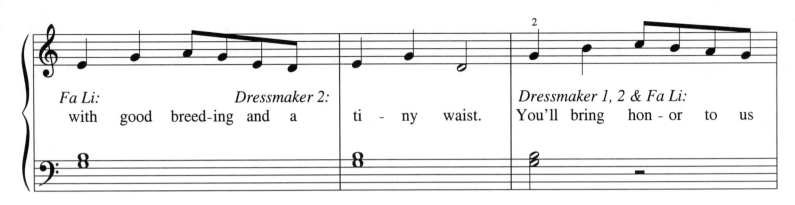

Fa Li: *Dressmaker 2:*
with   good   breed-ing   and   a   ti - ny   waist.   *Dressmaker 1, 2 & Fa Li:* You'll   bring   hon - or   to   us

all.   *Women:* We   all   must   serve   our

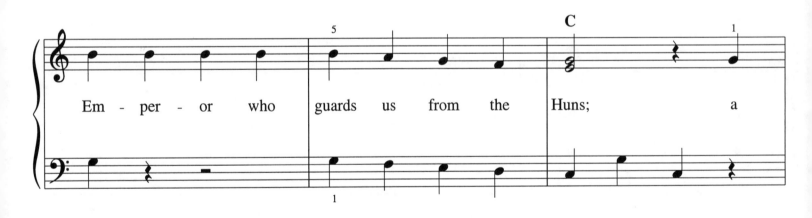

Em - per - or   who   guards   us   from   the   Huns;   a

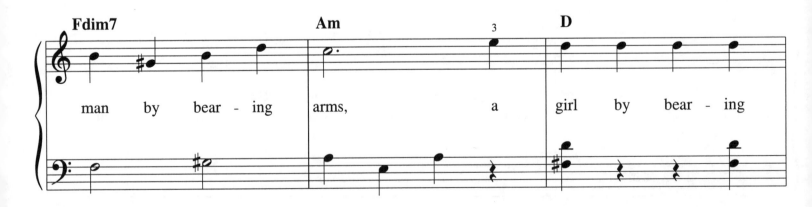

man   by   bear - ing   arms,   a   girl   by   bear - ing

sons.   When we're through,   you can't fail,

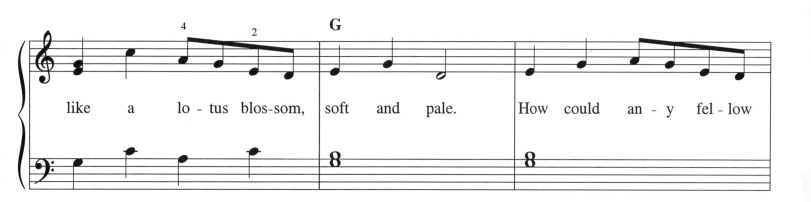

like a lo - tus blos-som,   soft and pale.   How could an - y fel - low

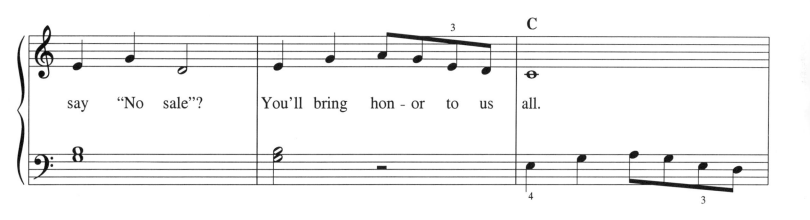

say "No sale"?   You'll bring hon - or to us   all.

Fa Li:
(Spoken:) There, you're ready.
smoothly

96

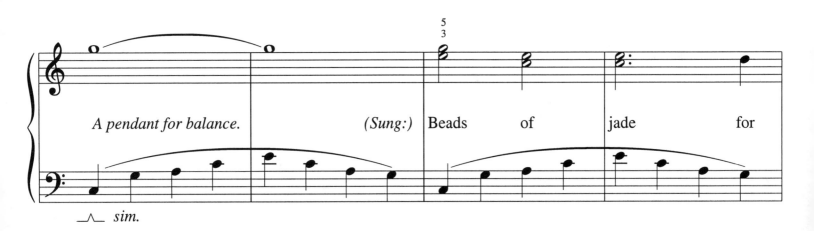

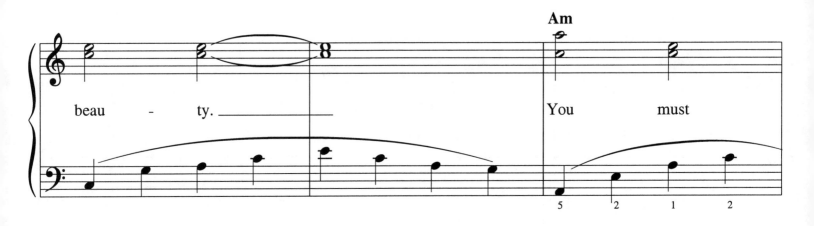

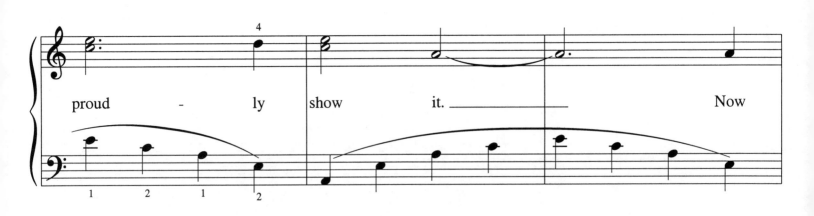

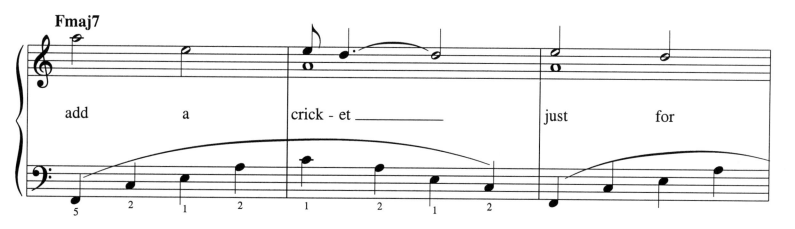

add   a   crick - et _____ just   for

luck   *and*   *e - ven*   *you*   *can't*   *blow*   *it.*

Mulan: An - ces - tors,   hear   my   plea.   Help   me   not   to   make   a

fool   of   me   and   to   not   up - root   my   fam - 'ly   tree.

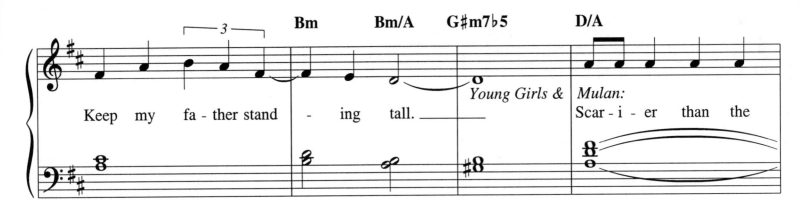

Keep my fa - ther stand - ing tall. _____

Young Girls & Mulan:
Scar - i - er than the

un - der - tak - er, we are meet - ing our match - mak - er.

All: Des - ti - ny guard our girls and our fu - ture as it

fast un - furls. Please look kind - ly on these cul - tured pearls,

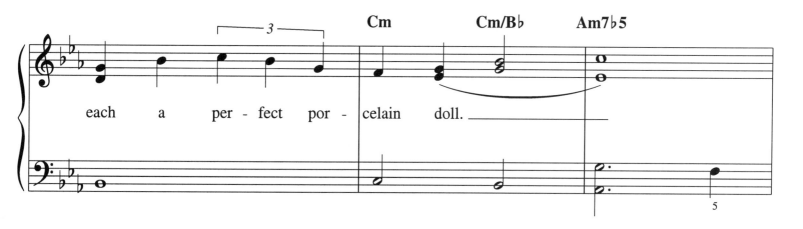

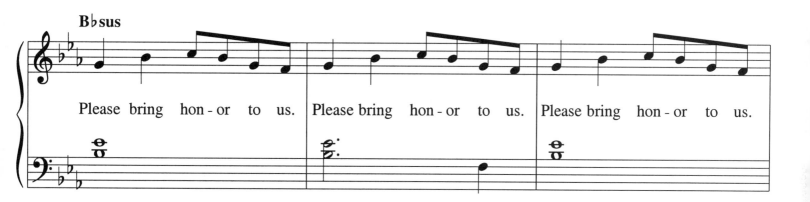

I LOVE TO LAUGH
from Walt Disney's MARY POPPINS

Words and Music by RICHARD M. SHERMAN
and ROBERT B. SHERMAN

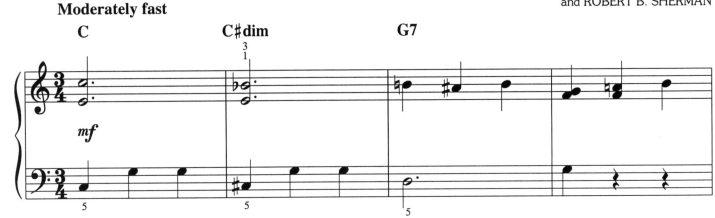

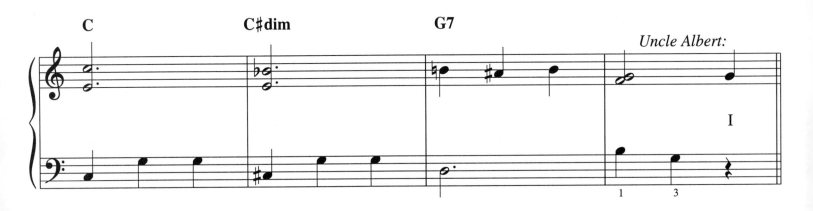

Uncle Albert:

I

love   to   laugh,   Ha!   Ha!   Ha!   Ha!

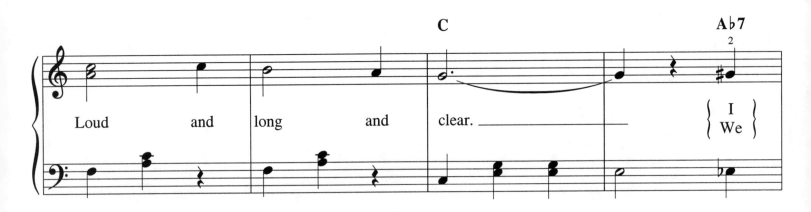

Loud   and   long   and   clear. _____

I
We

101

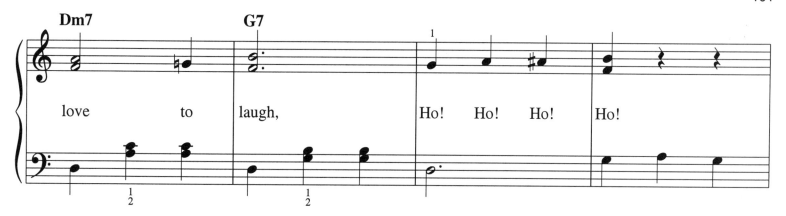

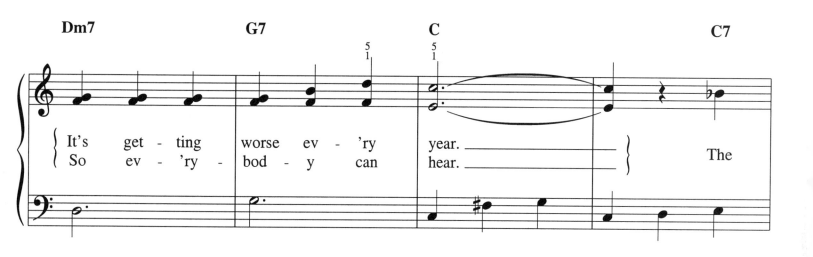

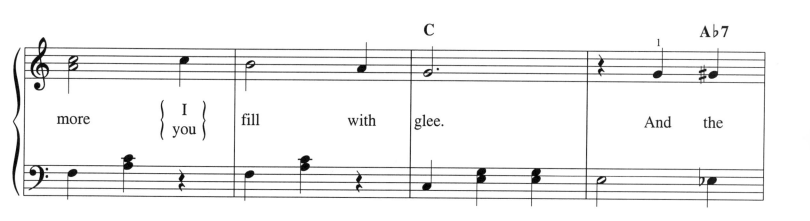

Dm7   G7

more   the   glee,   He!   He!   He!   He!   The

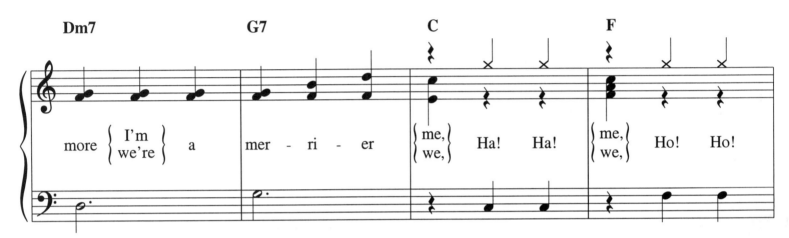

Dm7   G7   C   F

more { I'm / we're } a   mer - ri - er   { me, / we, }   Ha!   Ha!   { me, / we, }   Ho!   Ho!

C   F   Dm7   G7

{ me! / we! }   It's   em - bar - rass - ing!   The   more { I'm / we're } a   mer - ri - er

Interlude

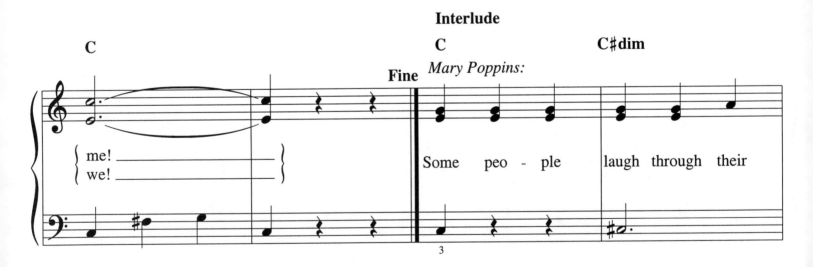

C   C   C#dim

Fine   *Mary Poppins:*

{ me! / we! }   Some   peo - ple   laugh through their

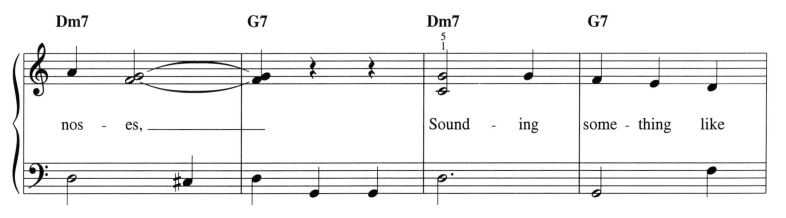

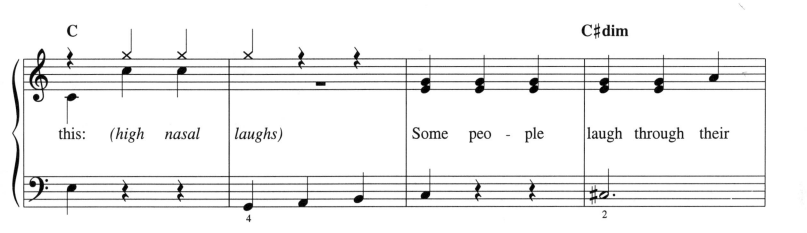

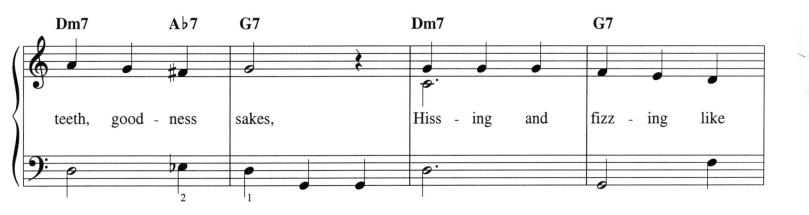

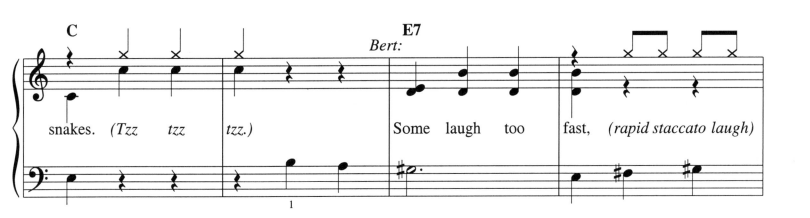

104

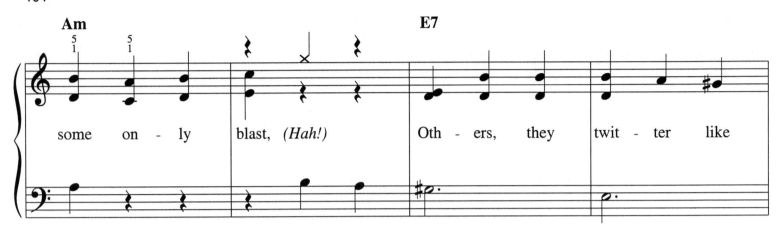

some on - ly blast, *(Hah!)* Oth - ers, they twit - ter like

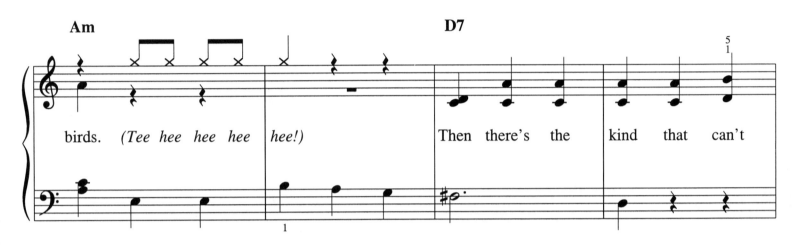

birds. *(Tee hee hee hee hee!)* Then there's the kind that can't

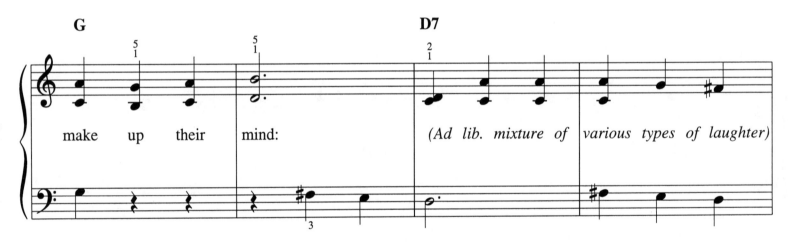

make up their mind: *(Ad lib. mixture of various types of laughter)*

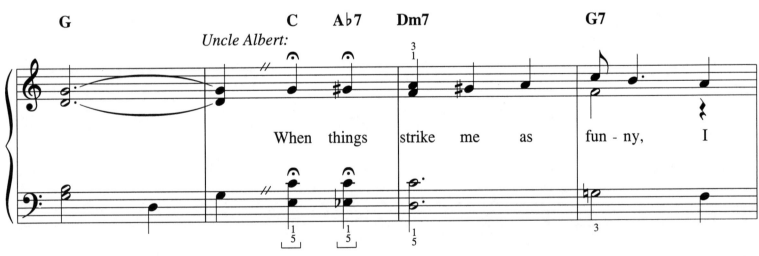

Uncle Albert:

When things strike me as fun - ny, I

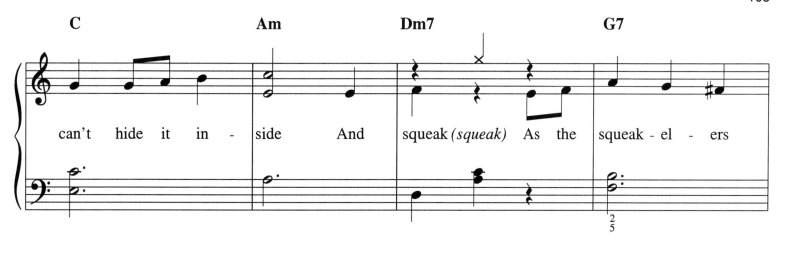

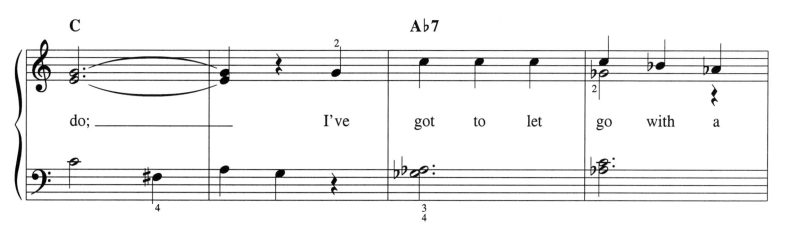

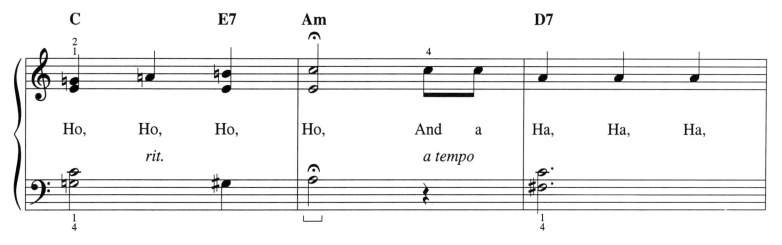

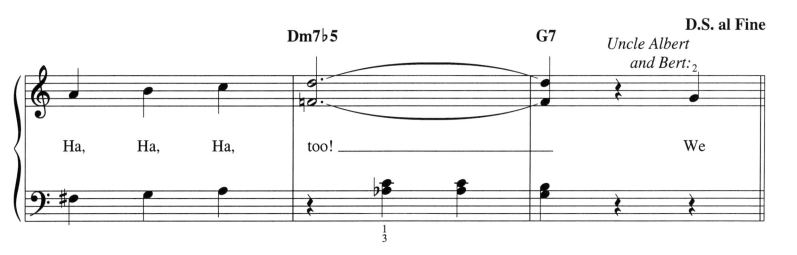

I WON'T SAY

(I'm in Love)
from Walt Disney Pictures' HERCULES

Music by ALAN MENKEN
Lyrics by DAVID ZIPPEL

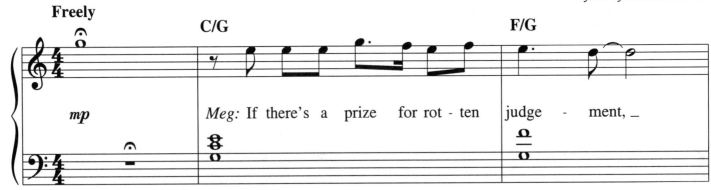

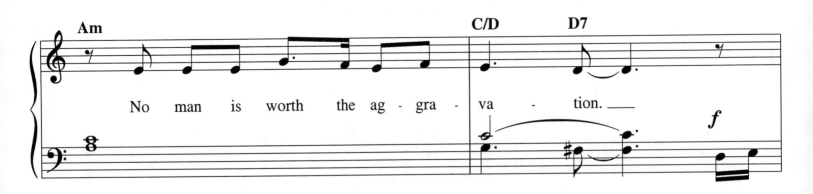

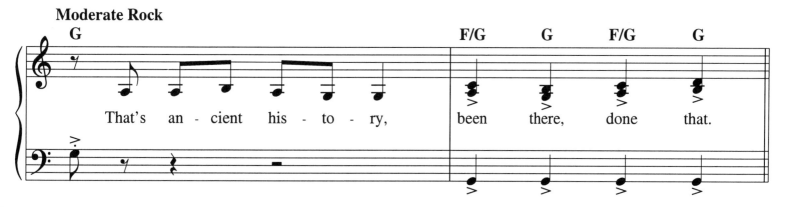

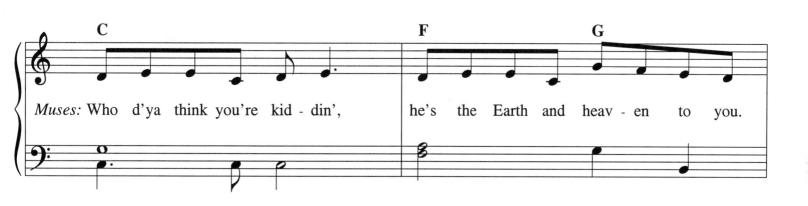

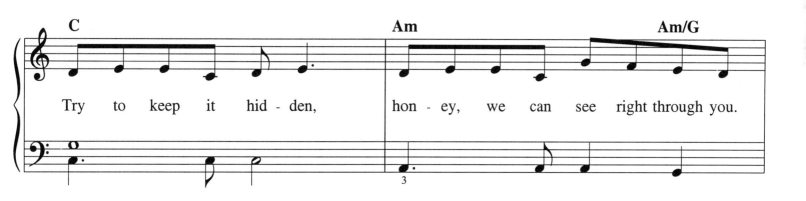

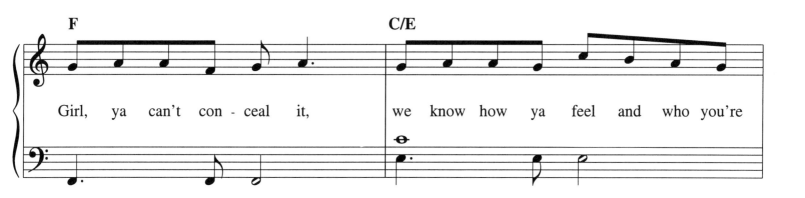

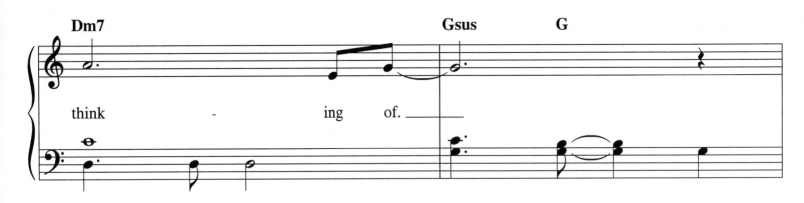

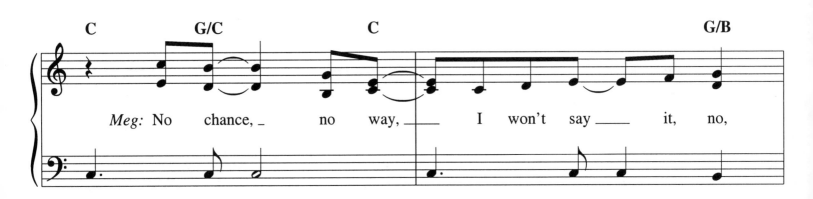

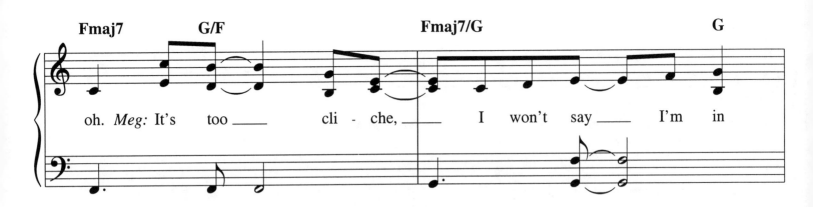

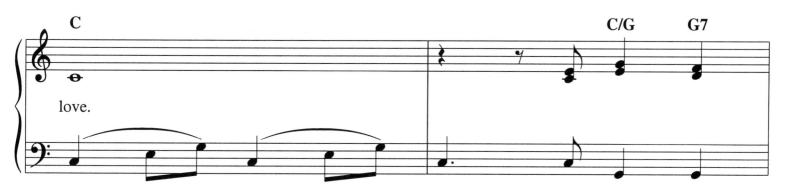

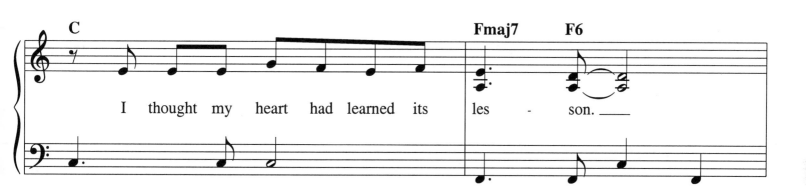

I thought my heart had learned its les - son. ____

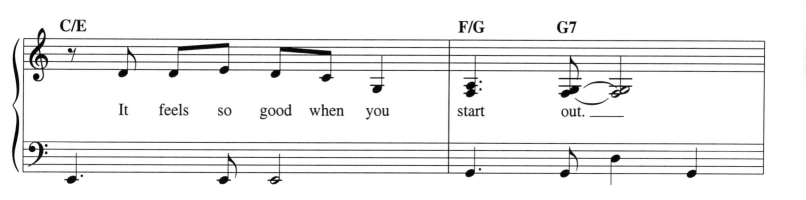

It feels so good when you start out. ____

My head is scream - ing, get a grip, girl, ____

110

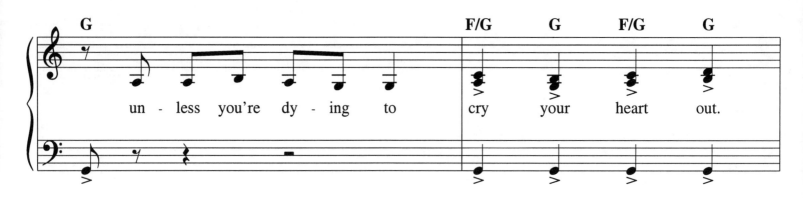

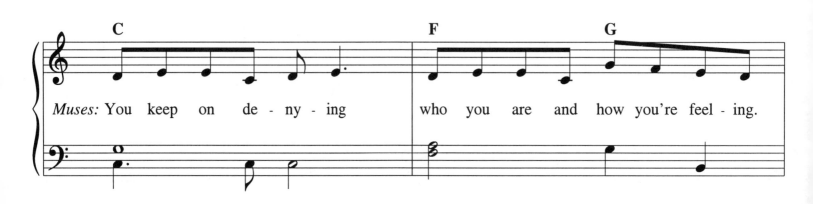

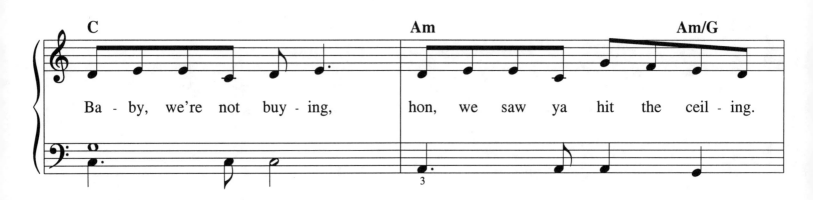

111

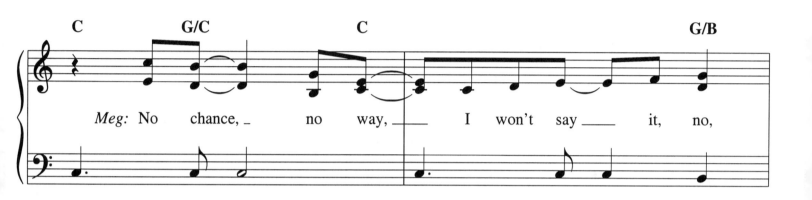

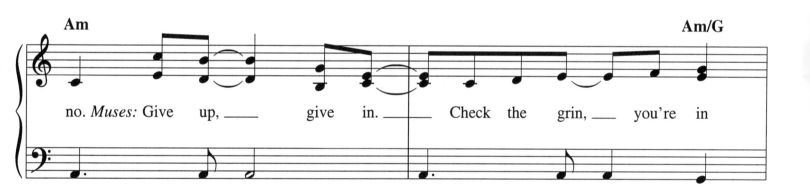

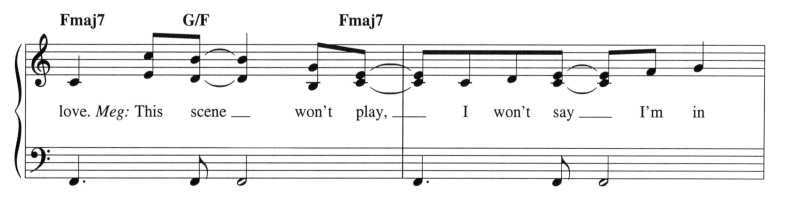

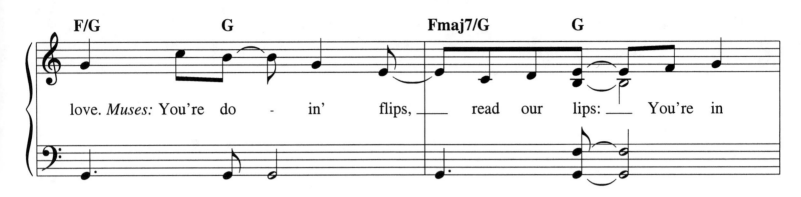

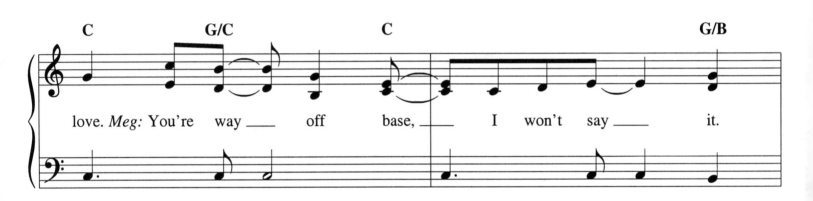

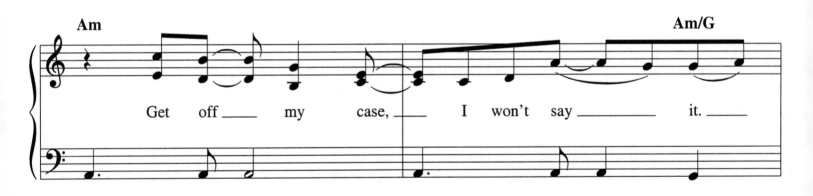

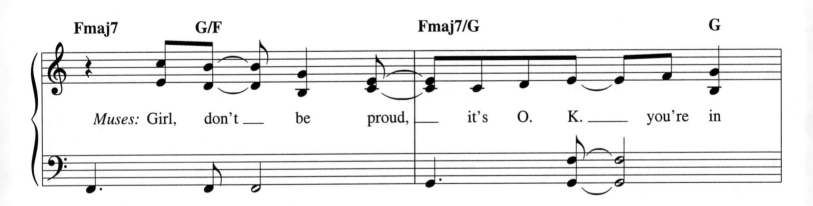

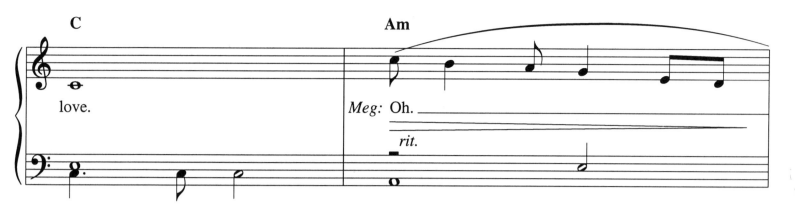

love.

Meg: Oh.

rit.

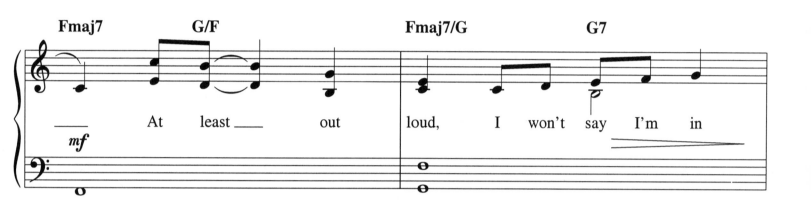

At least ___ out loud, I won't say I'm in

mf

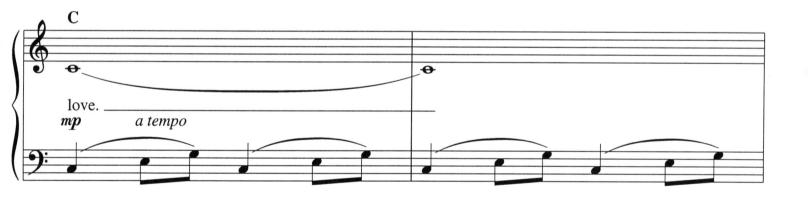

love. ___

mp   *a tempo*

rit.

I'M LATE
from Walt Disney's ALICE IN WONDERLAND

Words by BOB HILLIARD
Music by SAMMY FAIN

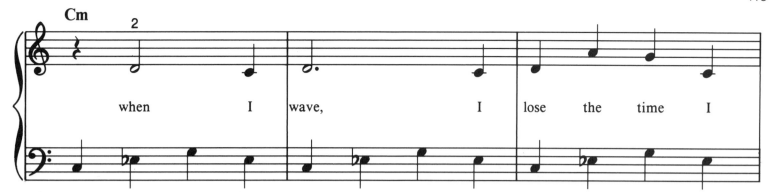

when I wave, I lose the time I

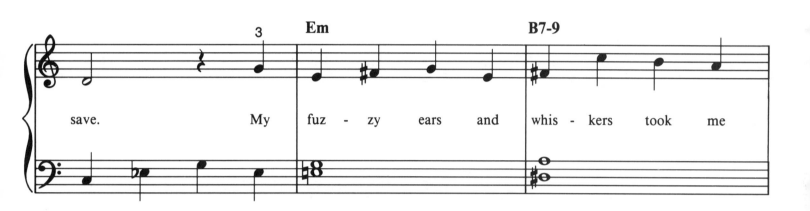

save. My fuz - zy ears and whis - kers took me

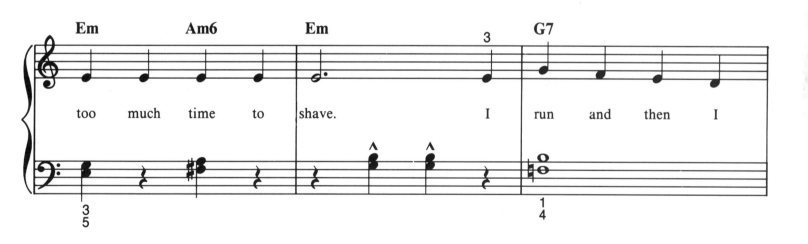

too much time to shave. I run and then I

hop, hop, hop, I wish that I could fly. There's

116

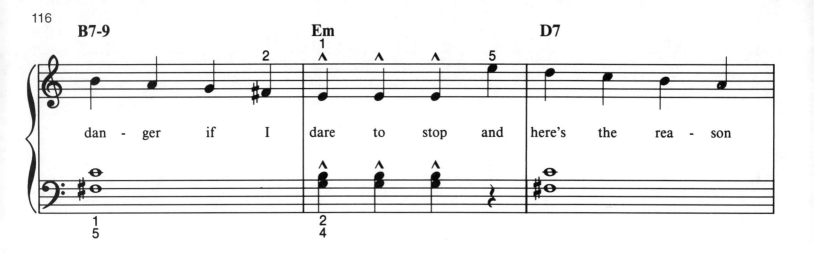

B7-9 ... **Em** ... **D7**

dan - ger if I | dare to stop and | here's the rea - son

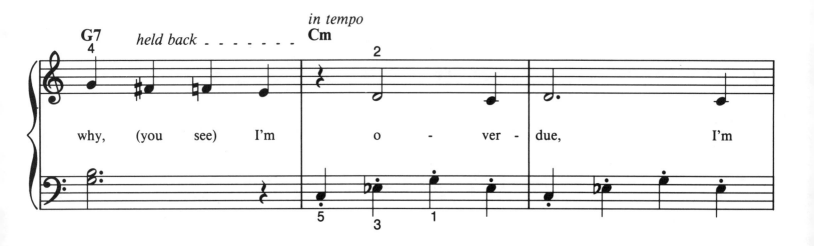

G7 *held back ....* *in tempo* **Cm**

why, (you see) I'm | o - ver - due, | I'm

D7 ... **C/G**

in a rab - bit | stew, Can't | e - ven say good -

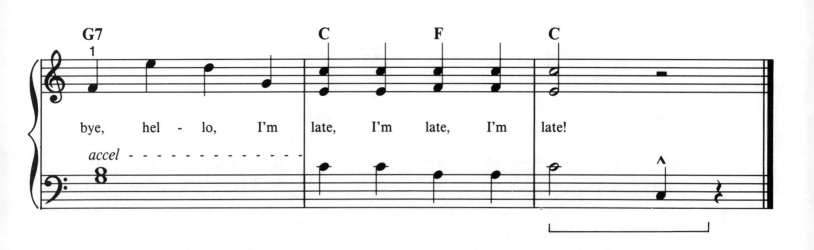

G7 ... **C** ... **F** ... **C**

bye, hel - lo, I'm | late, I'm late, I'm | late!

accel - - - - - - - - - - - - -

IT'S NOT EASY
from Walt Disney's PETE'S DRAGON

Words and Music by AL KASHA
and JOEL HIRSCHHORN

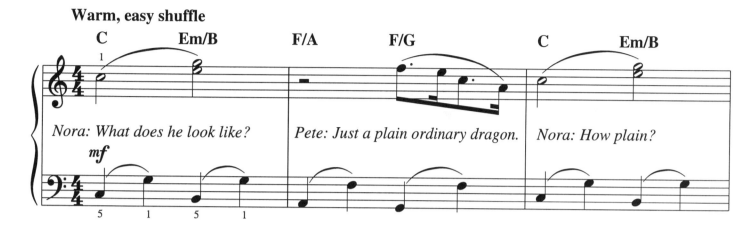

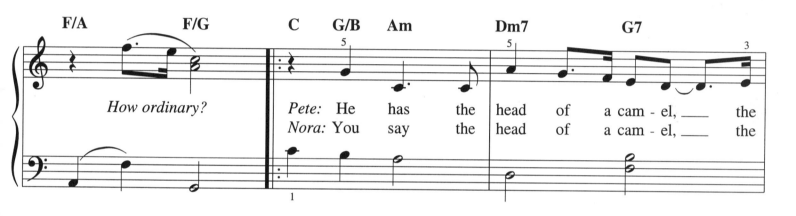

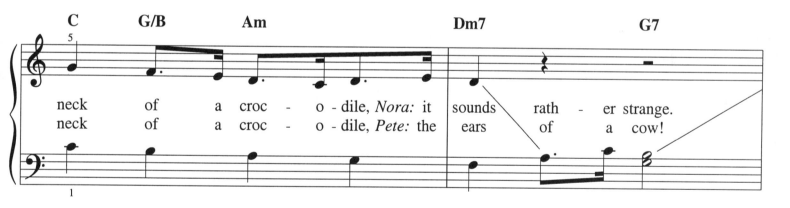

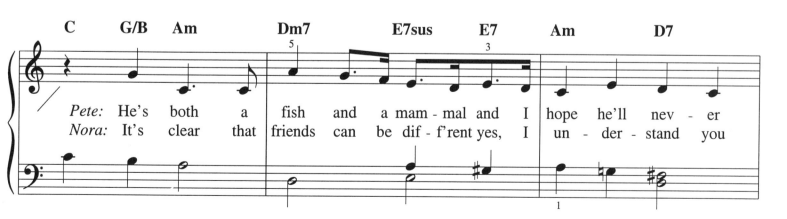

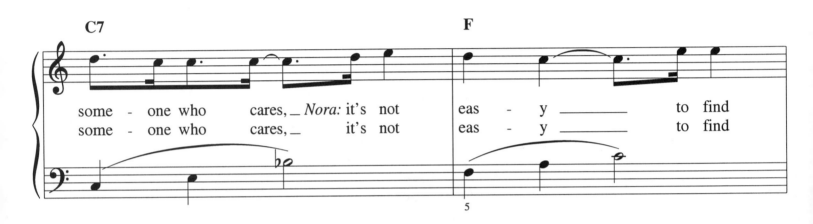

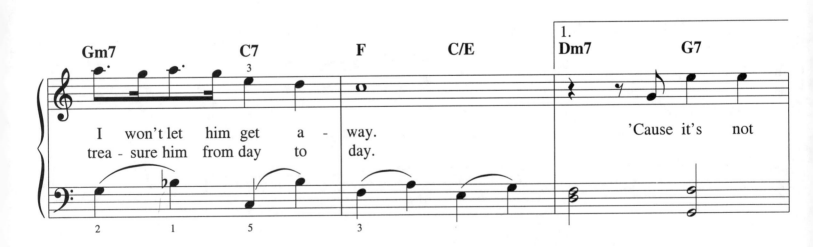

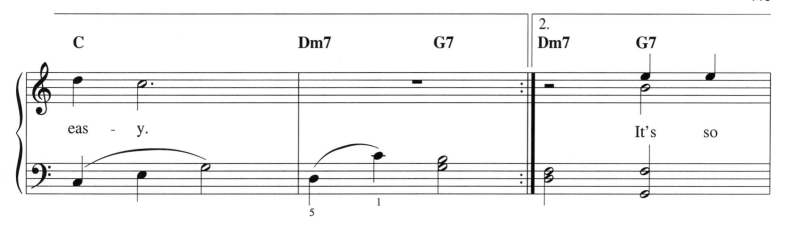

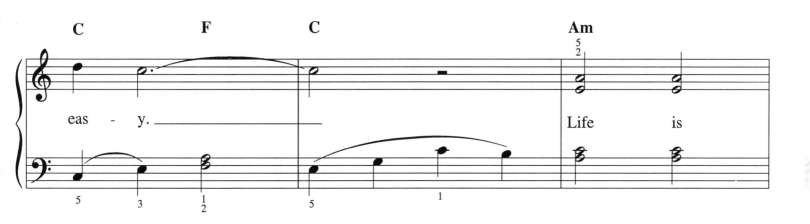

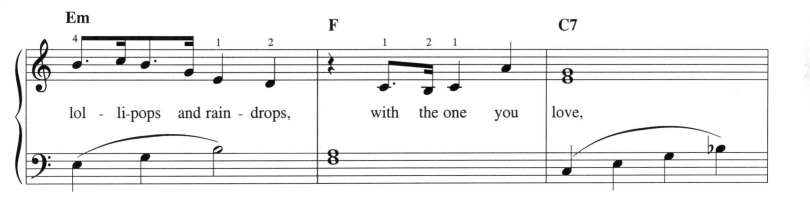

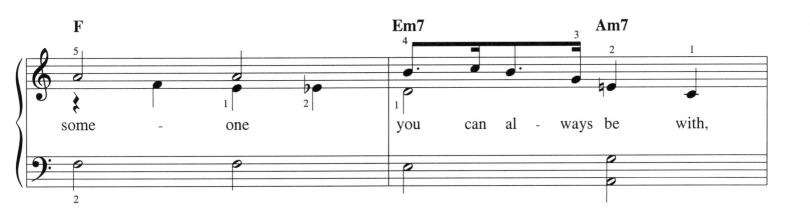

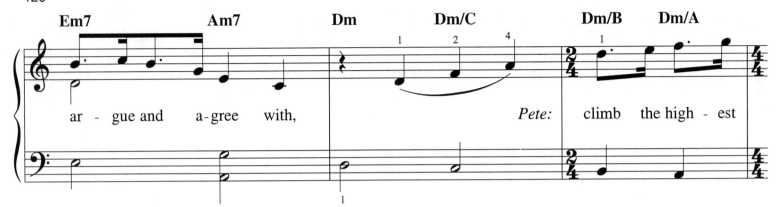

ar - gue and a-gree with, *Pete:* climb the high - est

tree with. *Both:* It's not eas - y _____ to share

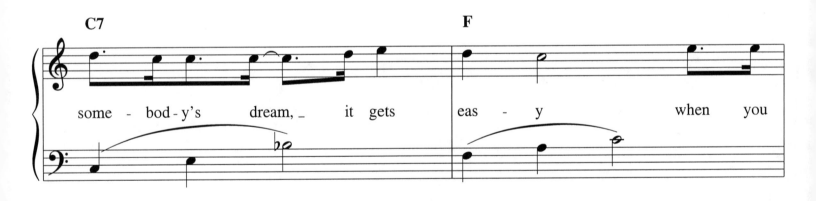

some - bod-y's dream, _ it gets eas - y when you

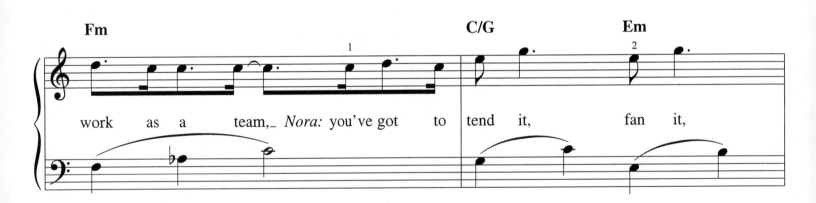

work as a team,_ *Nora:* you've got to tend it, fan it,

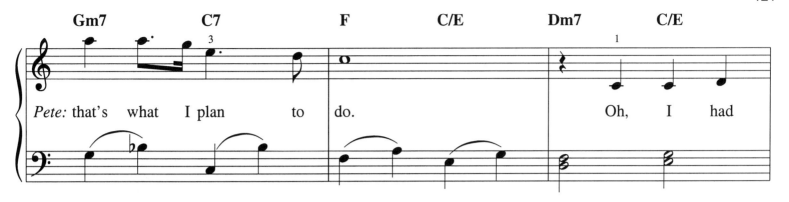

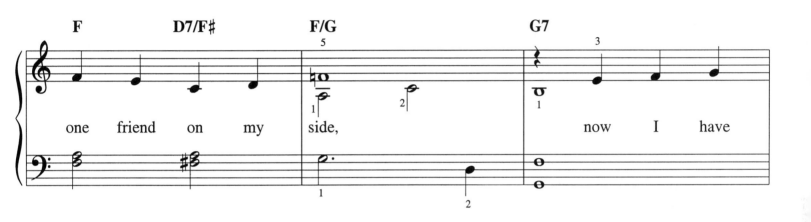

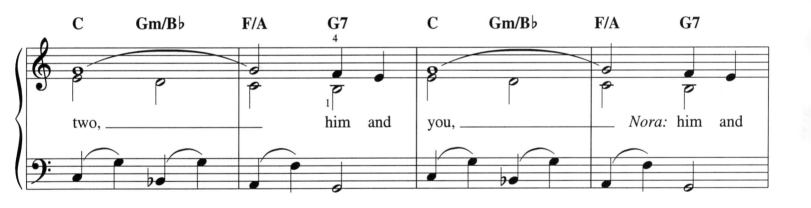

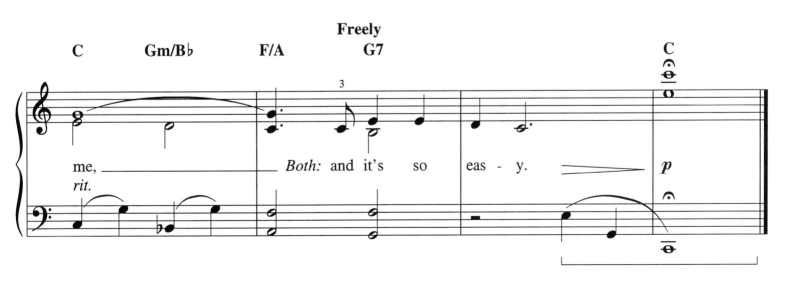

IF I NEVER KNEW YOU

(Love Theme from POCAHONTAS)
from Walt Disney's POCAHONTAS

Music by ALAN MENKEN
Lyrics by STEPHEN SCHWARTZ

Moderately

With pedal

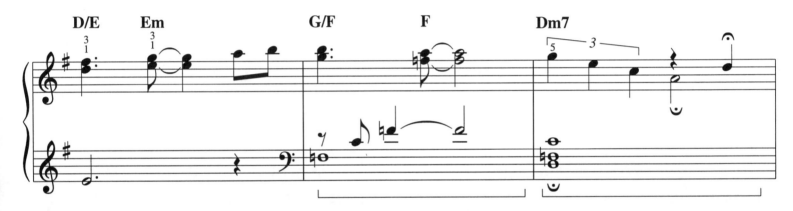

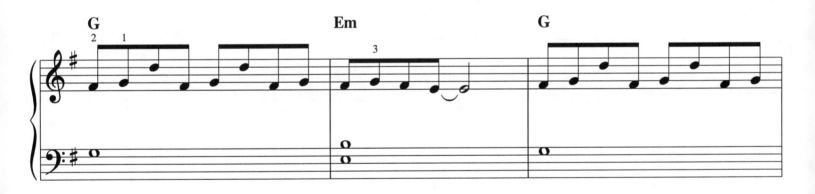

Male: If I nev - er knew you, —

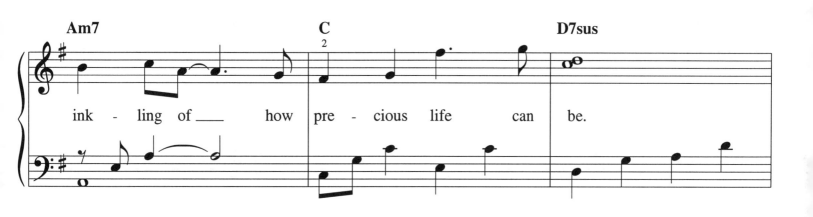

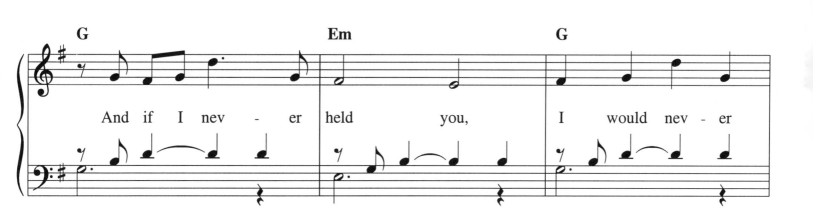

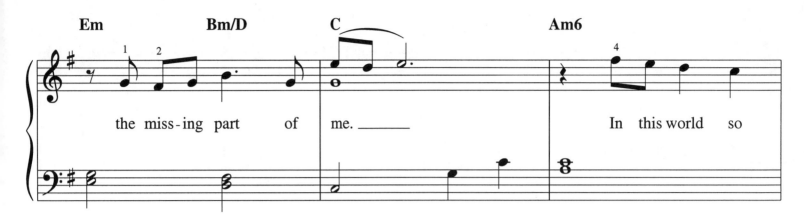

the miss-ing part of me. _____ In this world so

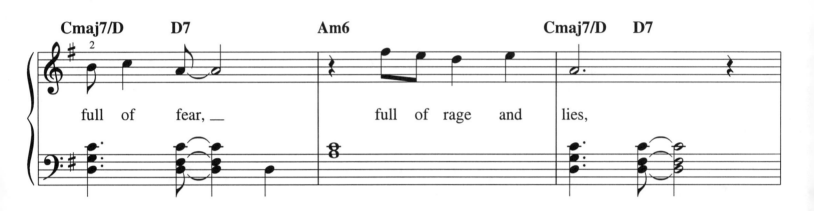

full of fear, _ full of rage and lies,

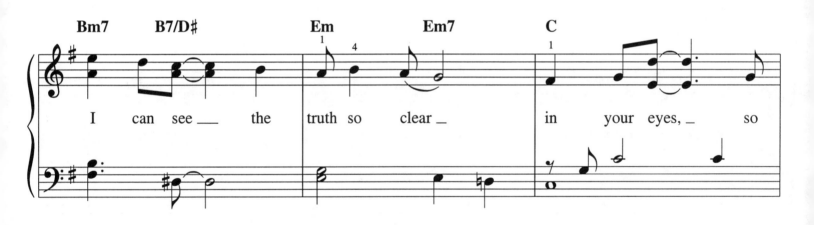

I can see _ the truth so clear _ in your eyes, _ so

dry your eyes. _ And I'm so grate - ful to you.

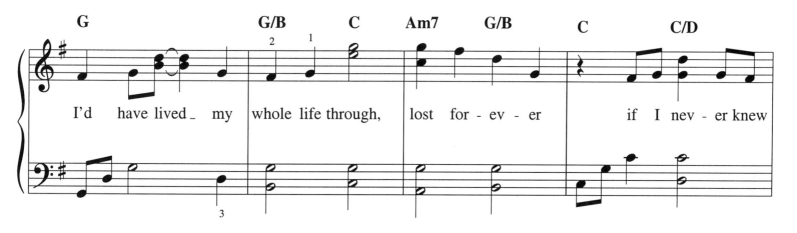

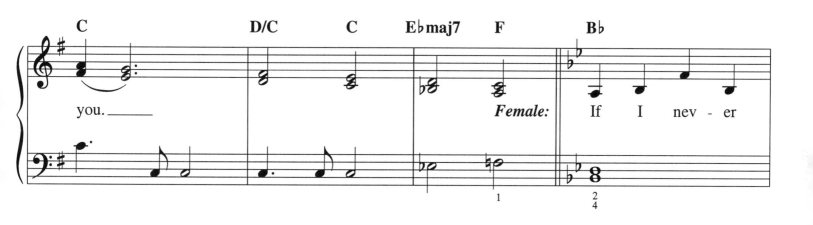

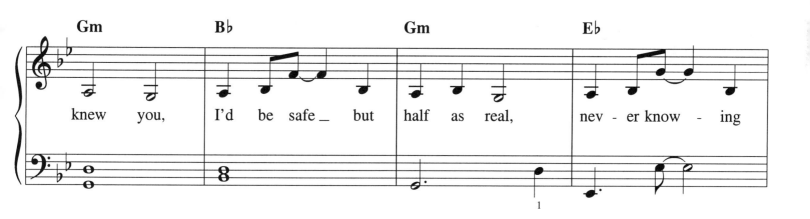

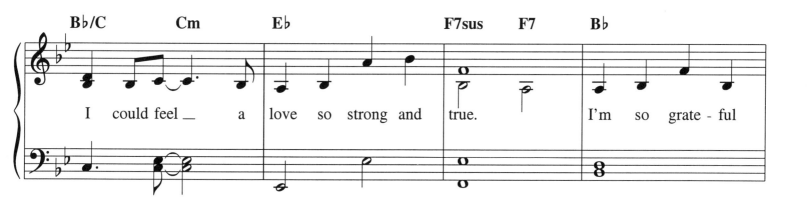

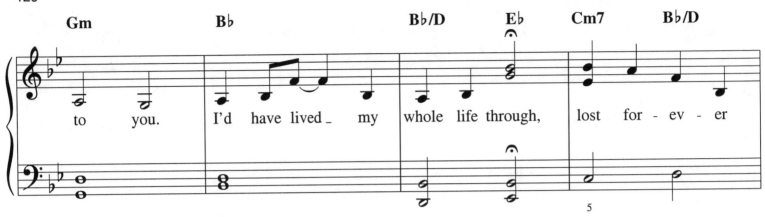

to you. I'd have lived _ my whole life through, lost for - ev - er

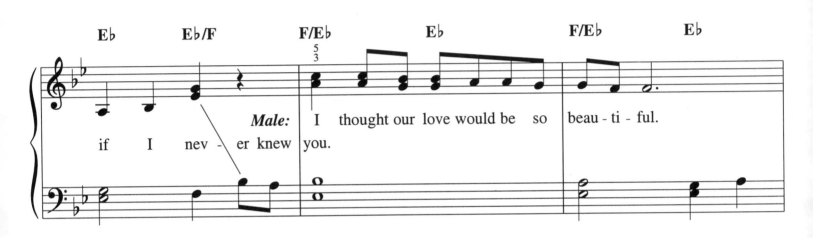

if I nev - er knew you. *Male:* I thought our love would be so beau - ti - ful.

Female: Some - how we'd make the whole world bright. _ *Both:* I nev - er knew that fear and

hate could be so strong, all they'd leave us were these whis-pers in the night, _ but

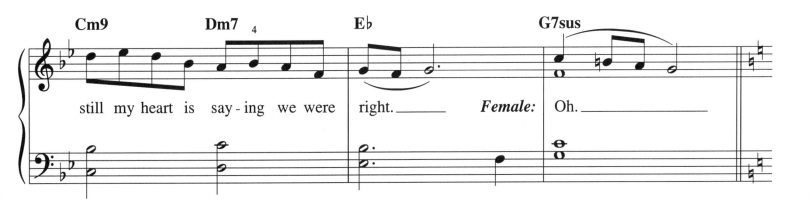

still my heart is say-ing we were right._____ *Female:* Oh._____

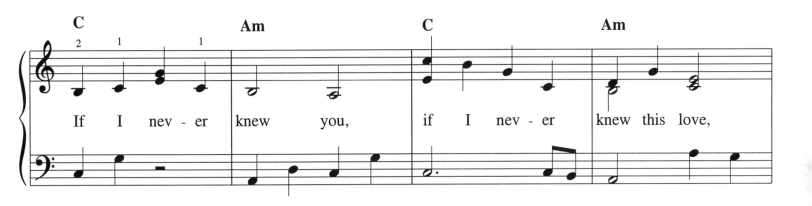

If I nev-er knew you, if I nev-er knew this love,

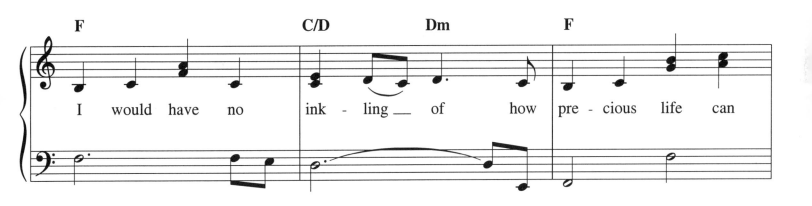

I would have no ink-ling ___ of how pre-cious life can

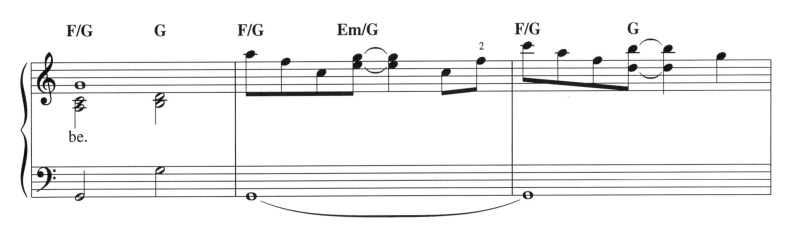

be.

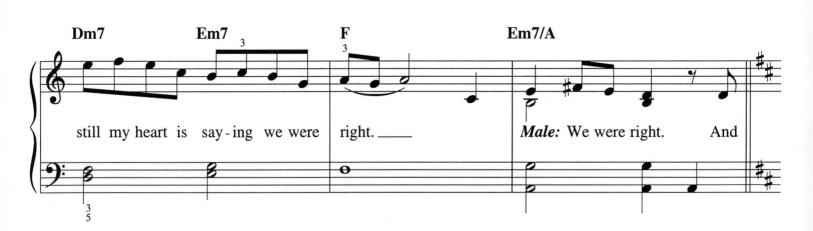

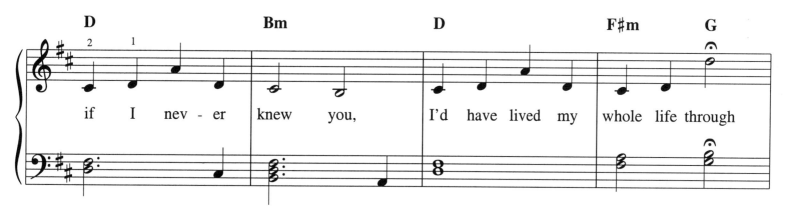

if I nev - er knew you, I'd have lived my whole life through

Female: emp - ty as ___ the sky, **Both:** nev - er know - ing

Freely

why, ___ lost for - ev - er if I nev - er knew you.

a tempo

rit.

IT'S A SMALL WORLD
from Disneyland and Walt Disney World's IT'S A SMALL WORLD

Words and Music by RICHARD M. SHERMAN
and ROBERT B. SHERMAN

It's a world of laugh - ter, a world of
There is just one moon and one gold - en
tears, It's a world of hopes and a world of
sun, And a smile means friend - ship to ev - 'ry -
fears. There's so much that we share that it's
one. Though the moun - tains di - vide and the o - ceans are
ware It's a small world af - ter all.
wide, It's a small world af - ter all.

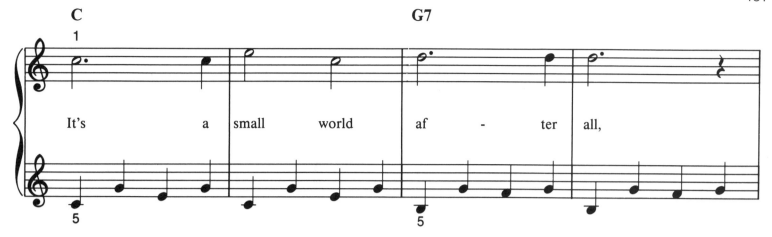

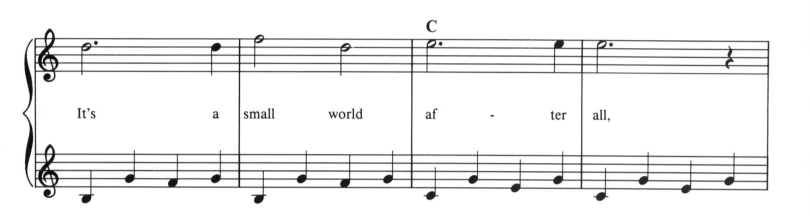

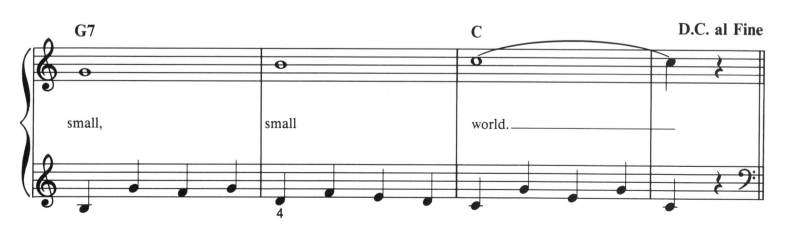

LAVENDER BLUE
(Dilly Dilly)
from Walt Disney's SO DEAR TO MY HEART

Words by LARRY MOREY
Music by ELIOT DANIEL

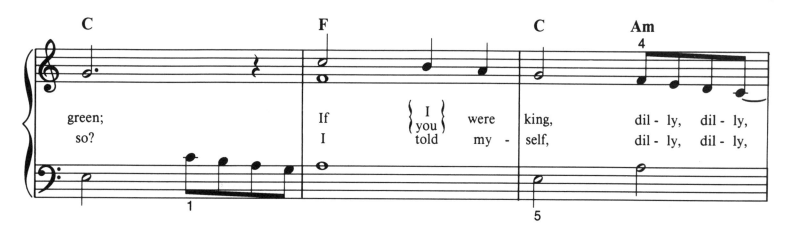

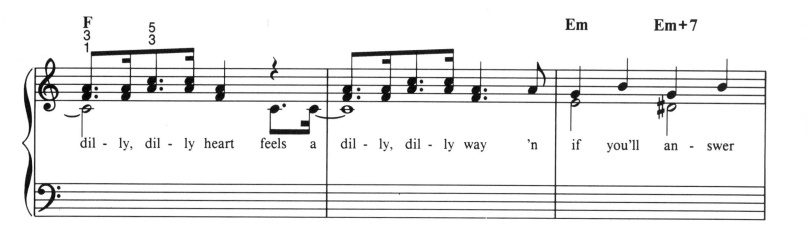

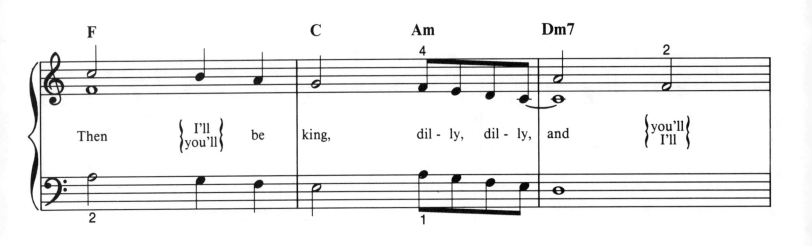

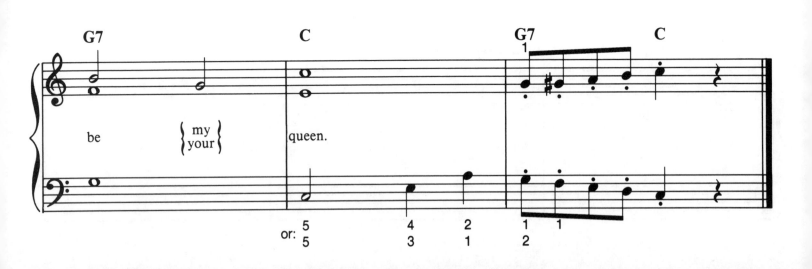

LITTLE APRIL SHOWER

from Walt Disney's BAMBI

Words by LARRY MOREY
Music by FRANK CHURCHILL

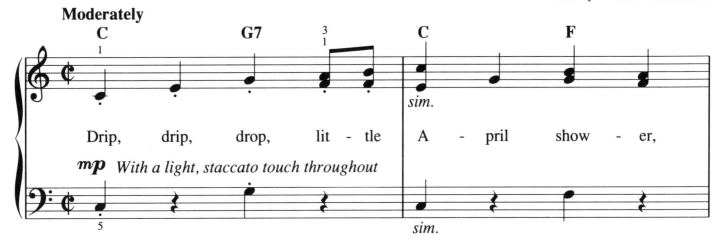

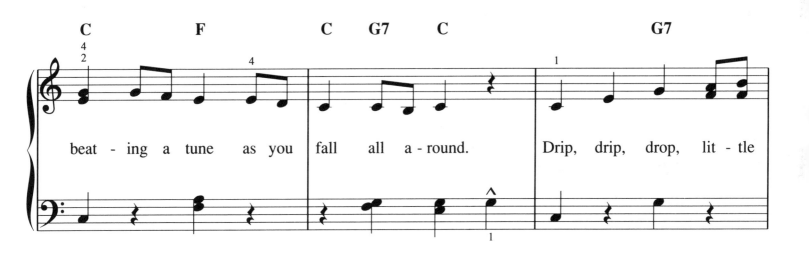

136

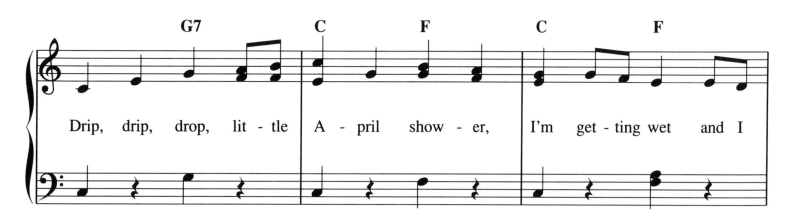

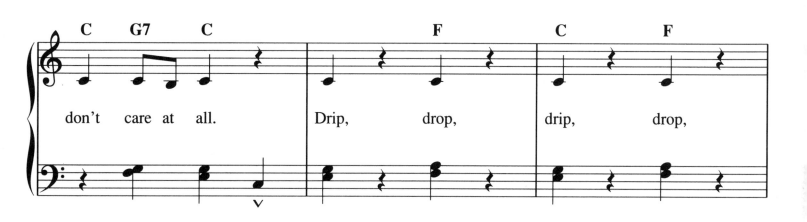

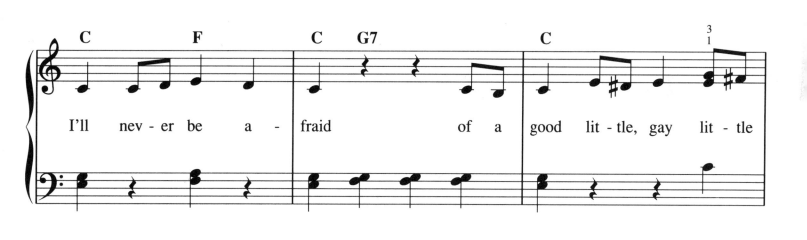

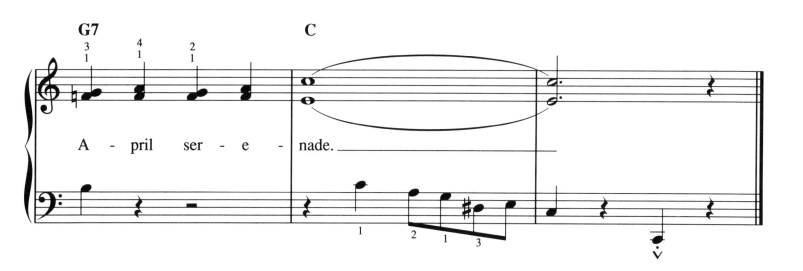

LET'S GET TOGETHER

from Walt Disney Pictures' THE PARENT TRAP

Words and Music by RICHARD M. SHERMAN
and ROBERT B. SHERMAN

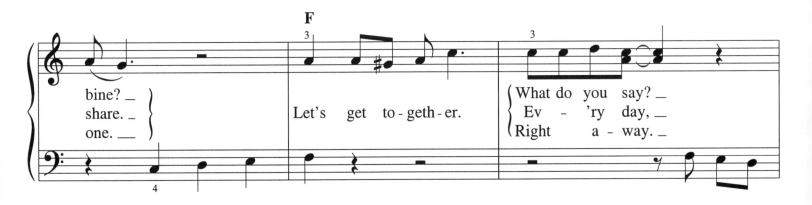

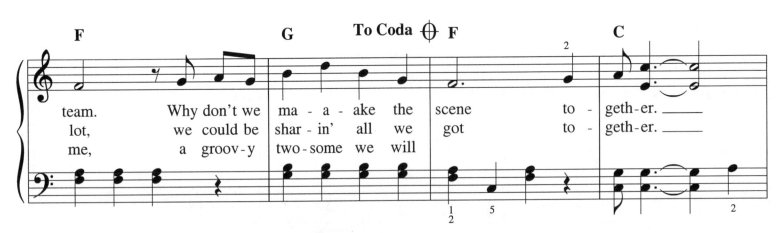

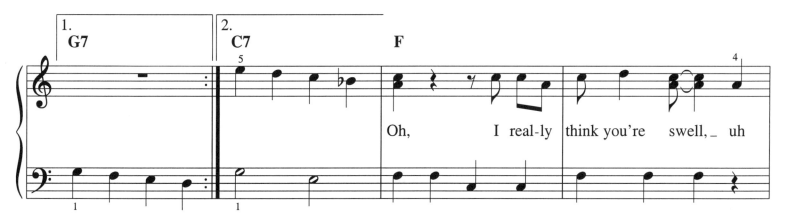

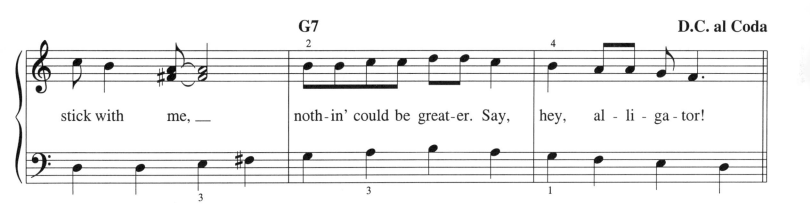

LISTEN WITH YOUR HEART

from Walt Disney's POCAHONTAS

Music by ALAN MENKEN
Lyrics by STEPHEN SCHWARTZ

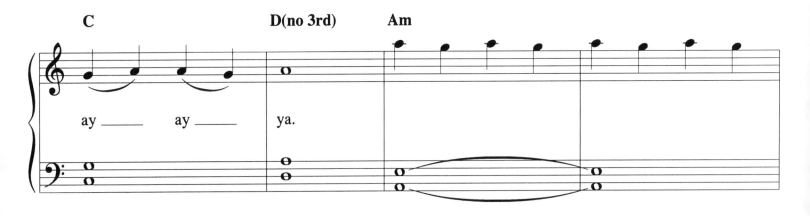

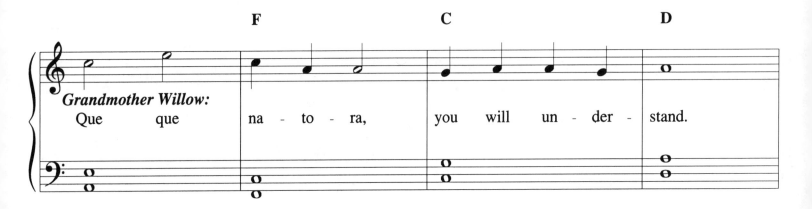

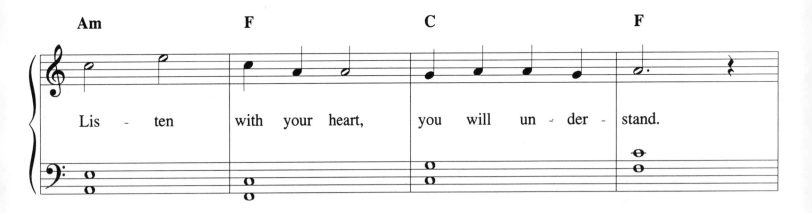

Let it break up - on you like a wave up - on the

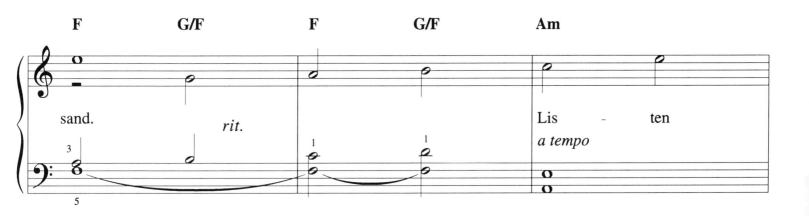

sand. *rit.* Lis - ten *a tempo*

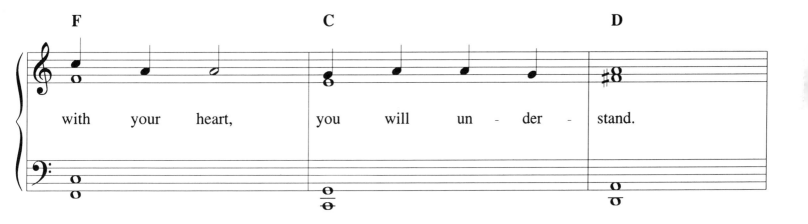

with your heart, you will un - der - stand.

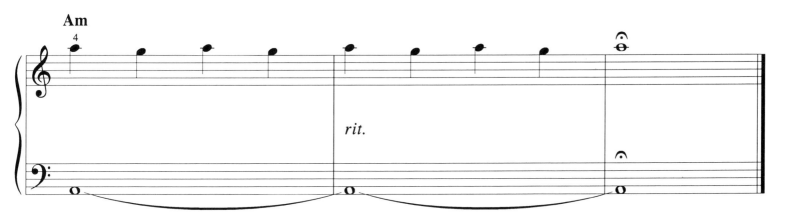

rit.

THE LORD IS GOOD TO ME

from Walt Disney's MELODY TIME

Words and Music by KIM GANNON
and WALTER KENT

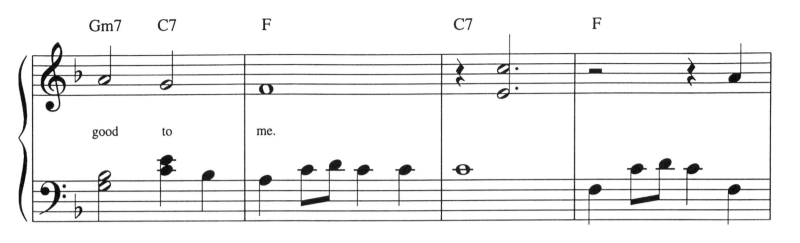

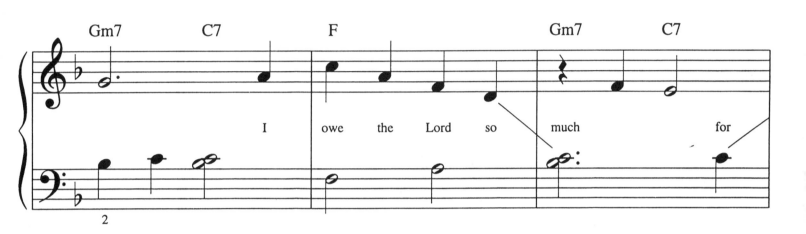

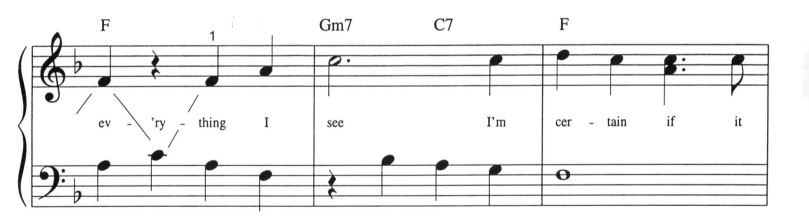

145

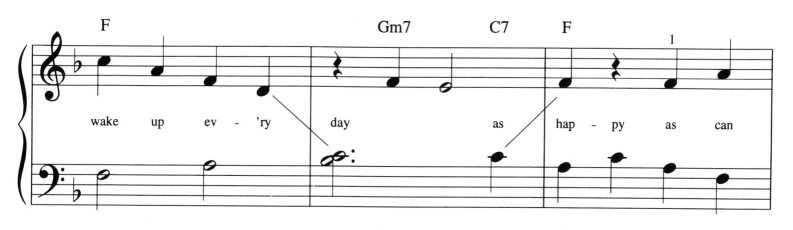

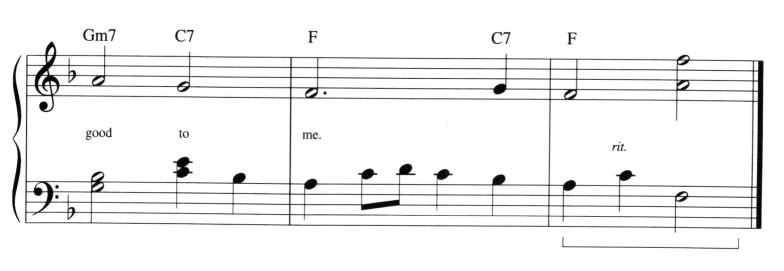

MICKEY MOUSE MARCH

from Walt Disney's THE MICKEY MOUSE CLUB

Words and Music by
JIMMIE DODD

147

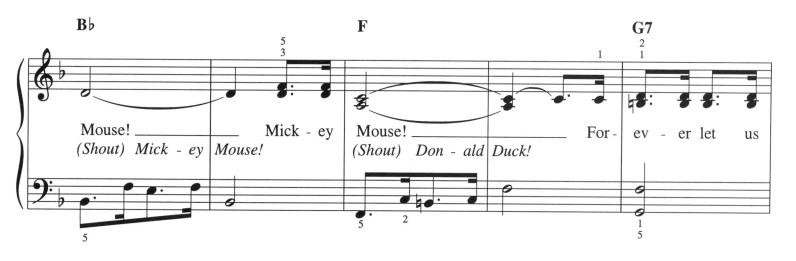

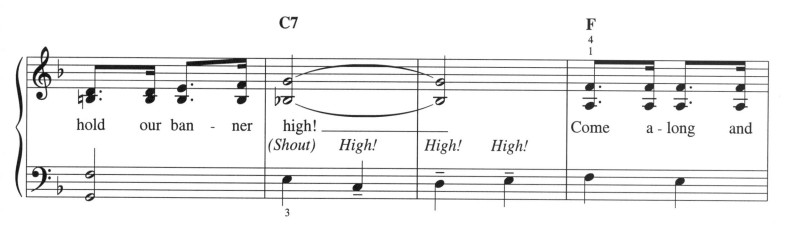

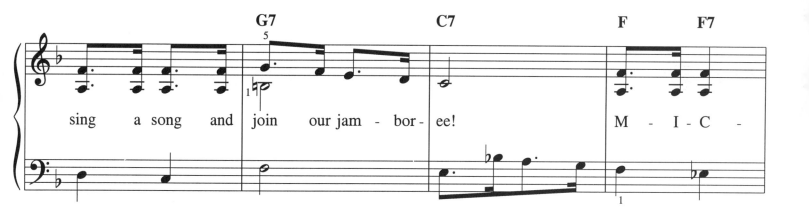

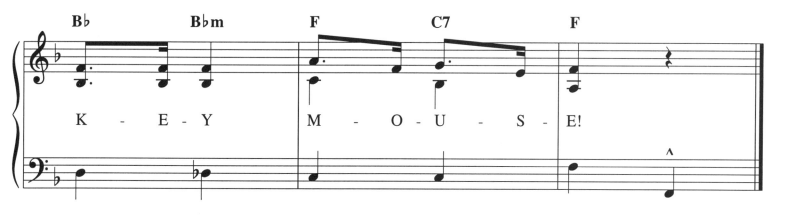

NEVER SMILE AT A CROCODILE

from Walt Disney's PETER PAN

Words by JACK LAWRENCE
Music by FRANK CHURCHILL

Moderately slow (Allegretto)

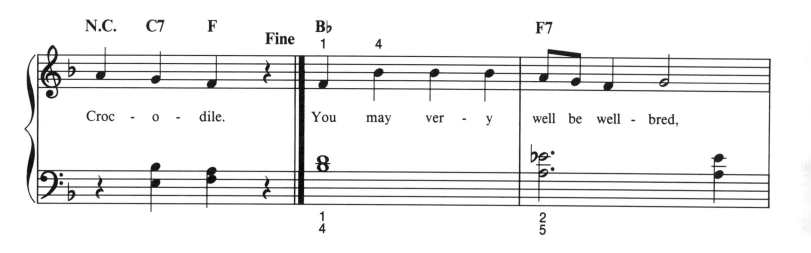

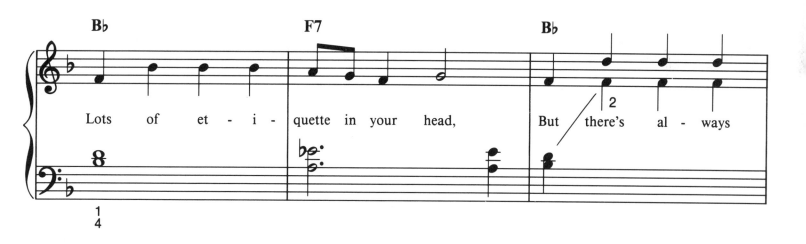

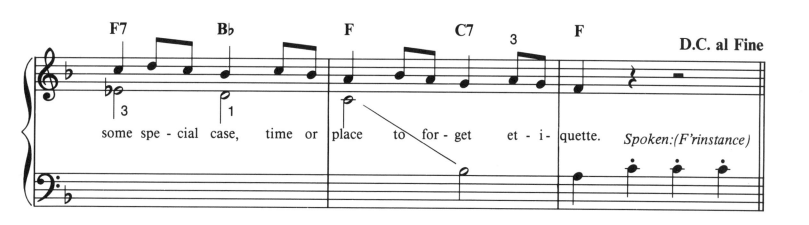

ONCE UPON A DREAM

from Walt Disney's SLEEPING BEAUTY

Words and Music by SAMMY FAIN
and JACK LAWRENCE
Adapted from a Theme by TCHAIKOVSKY

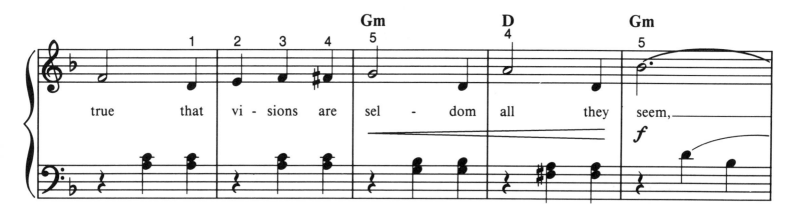

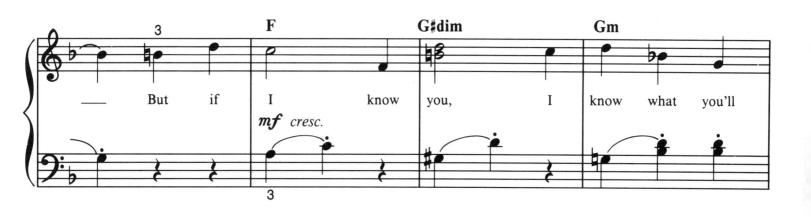

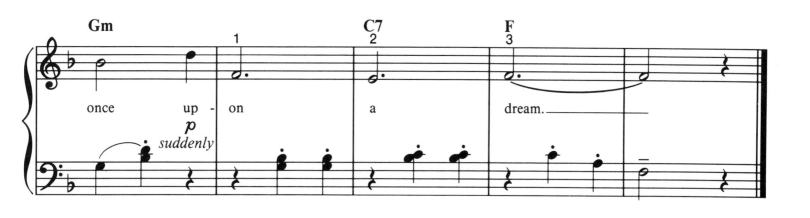

OO-DE-LALLY

from Walt Disney's ROBIN HOOD

Words and Music by
ROGER MILLER

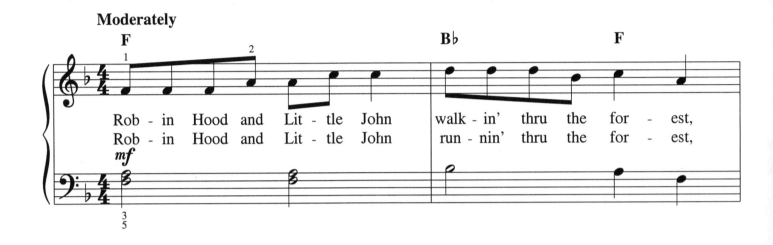

Rob - in Hood and Lit - tle John walk - in' thru the for - est,
Rob - in Hood and Lit - tle John run - nin' thru the for - est,

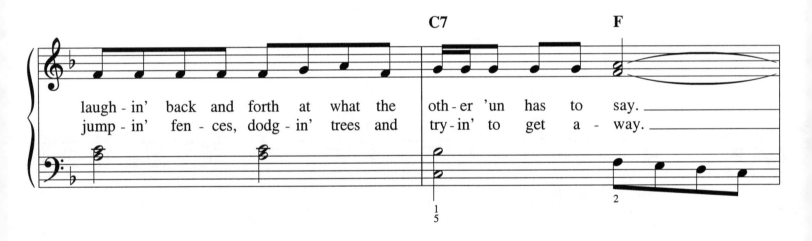

laugh - in' back and forth at what the oth - er 'un has to say.
jump - in' fen - ces, dodg - in' trees and try - in' to get a - way.

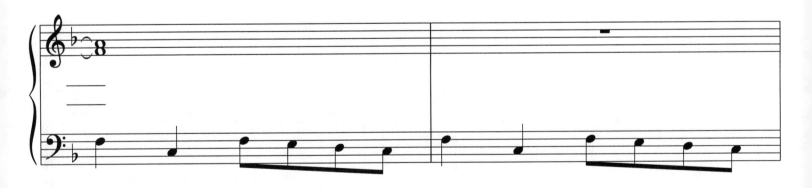

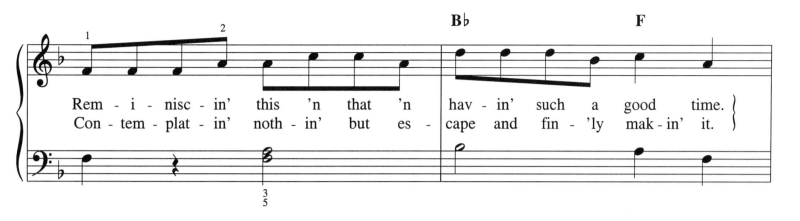

Rem - i - nisc - in' this 'n that 'n hav - in' such a good time.
Con - tem - plat - in' noth - in' but es - cape and fin - 'ly mak - in' it.

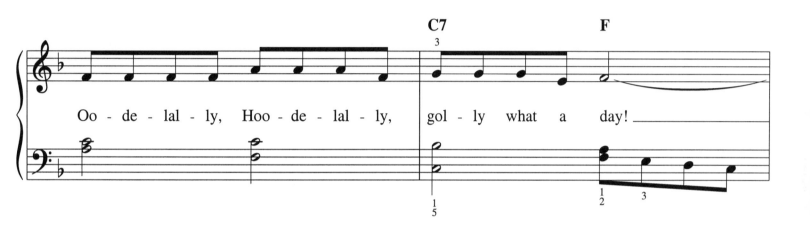

Oo - de - lal - ly, Hoo - de - lal - ly, gol - ly what a day! ____

To Coda ⊕

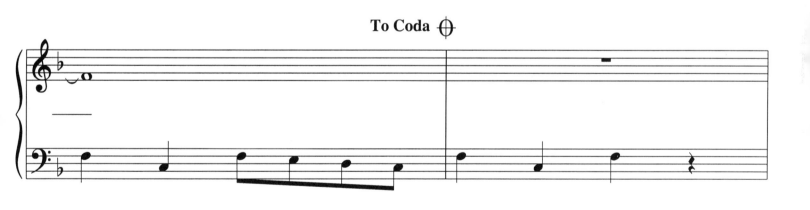

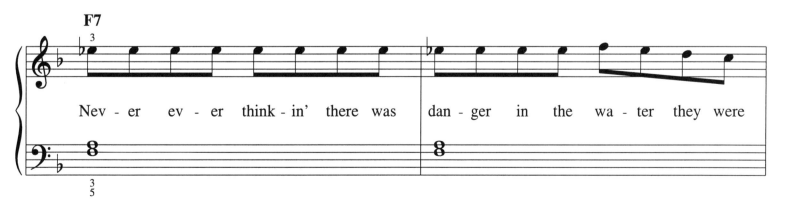

Nev - er ev - er think - in' there was dan - ger in the wa - ter they were

drink - in', they just guz - zled it down.

Nev - er dream - in' that a schem - in' sher - iff and his pos - se was a

D.C. al Coda

watch - in' them and gath - er - in' a - round.

CODA

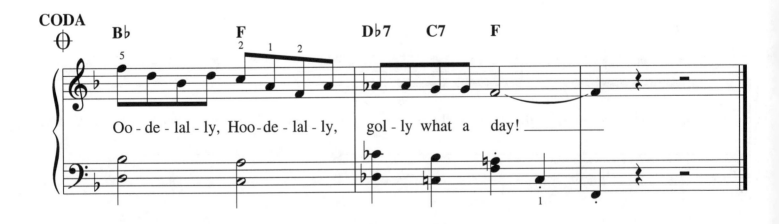

Oo - de - lal - ly, Hoo - de - lal - ly, gol - ly what a day!

REFLECTION
from Walt Disney Pictures' MULAN

Music by MATTHEW WILDER
Lyrics by DAVID ZIPPEL

I were tru - ly to be my-self, I would break my fam - 'ly's

heart. Who is that

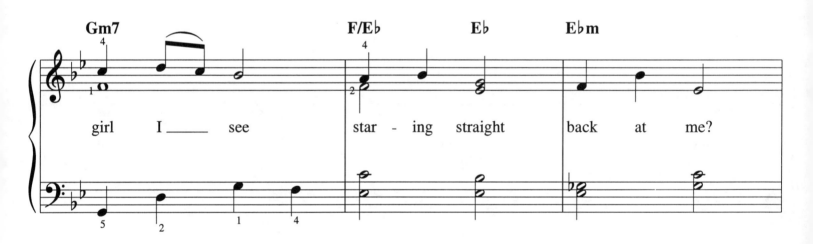

girl I ____ see star - ing straight back at me?

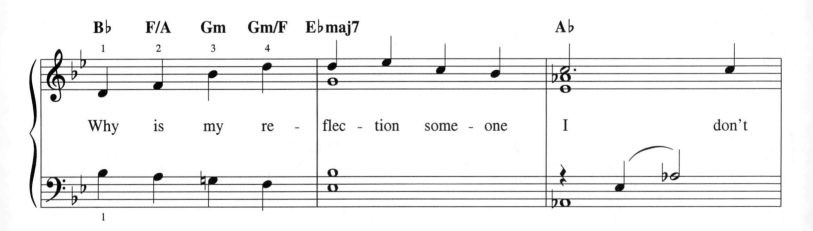

Why is my re - flec - tion some - one I don't

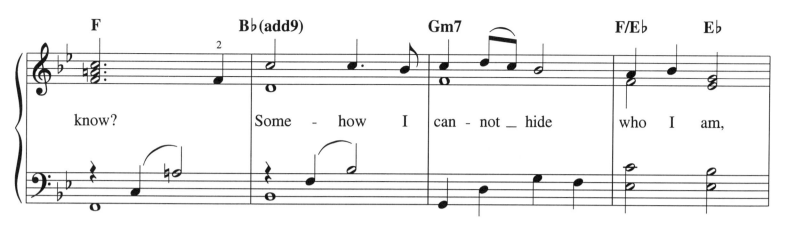

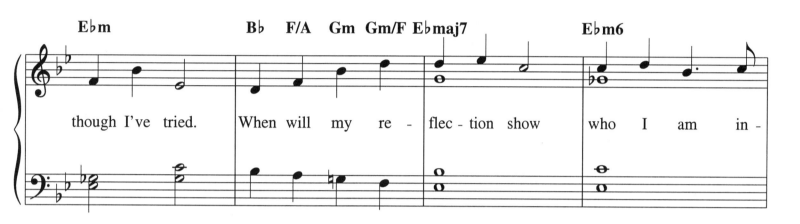

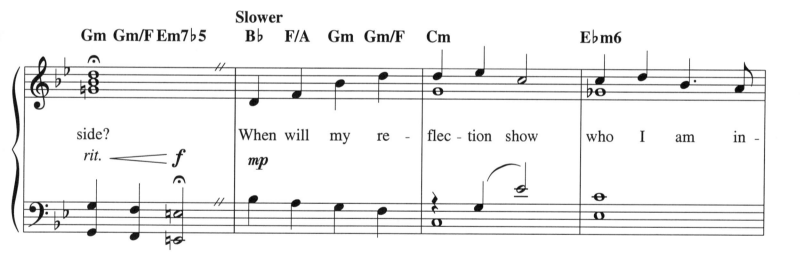

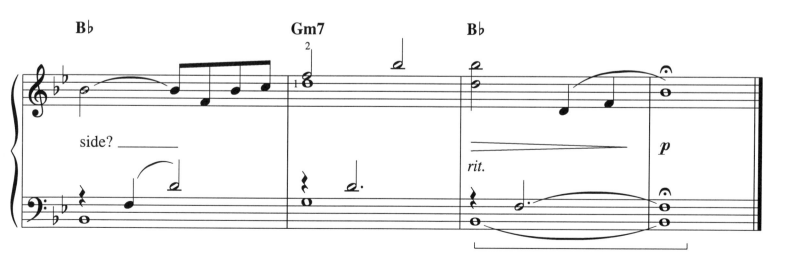

PART OF YOUR WORLD
from Walt Disney's THE LITTLE MERMAID

Lyrics by HOWARD ASHMAN
Music by ALAN MENKEN

Look at this stuff. _

Is - n't it neat? _   Would-n't you think _   my col - lec-tion's com-plete?_

Would-n't you think _   I'm the girl,   the girl who has   ev - 'ry -thing. _

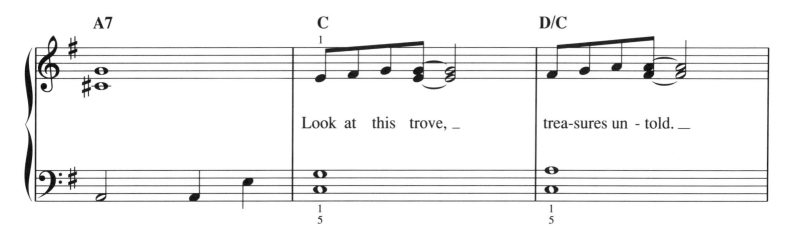

Look at this trove, _ trea-sures un - told. _

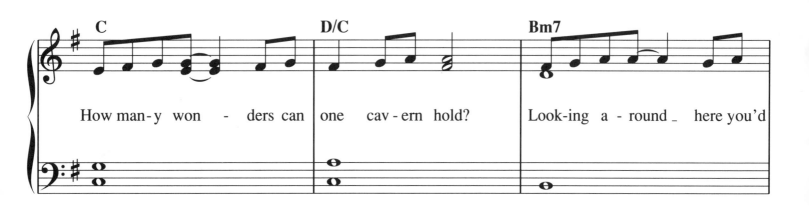

How man-y won - ders can one cav-ern hold? Look-ing a - round _ here you'd

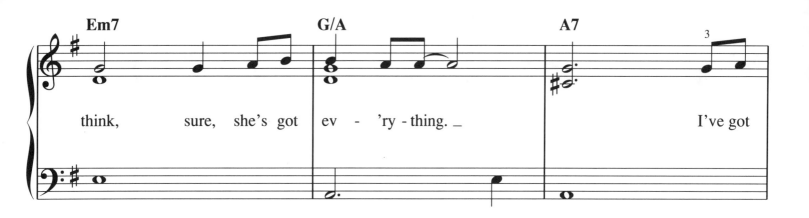

think, sure, she's got ev - 'ry-thing. _ I've got

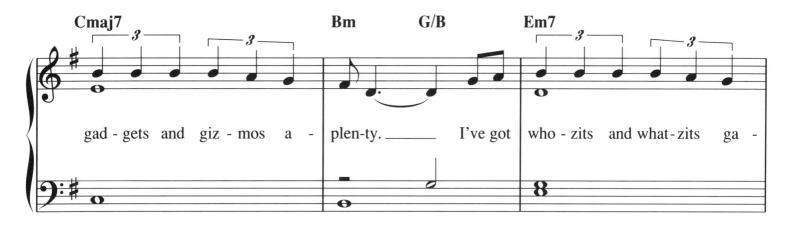

gad - gets and giz-mos a - plen-ty. _ I've got who - zits and what-zits ga -

160

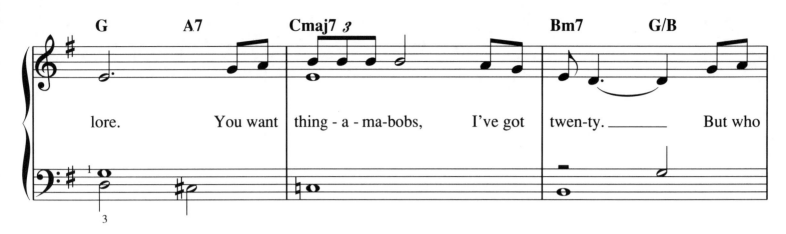

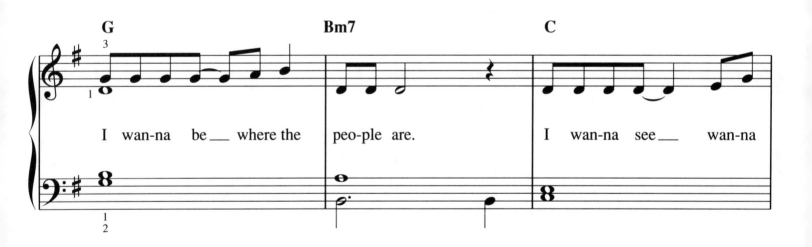

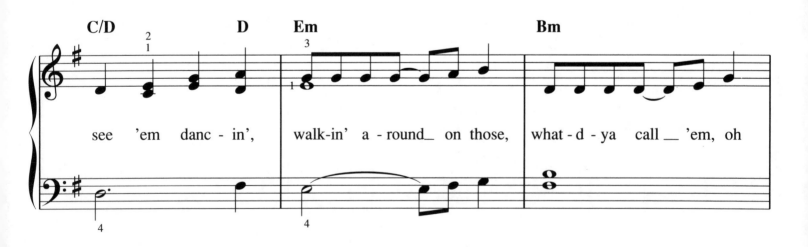

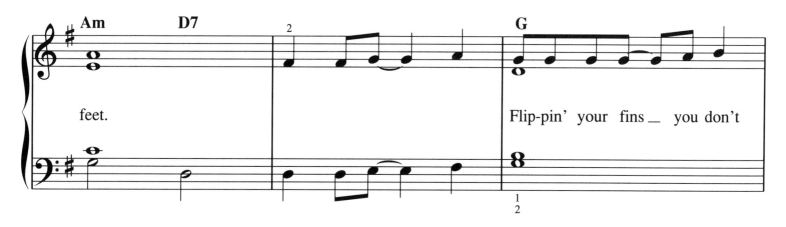

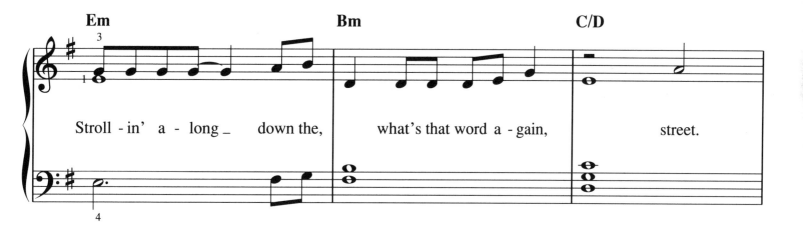

stay all day in the sun. Wan - der - in' free, wish I could

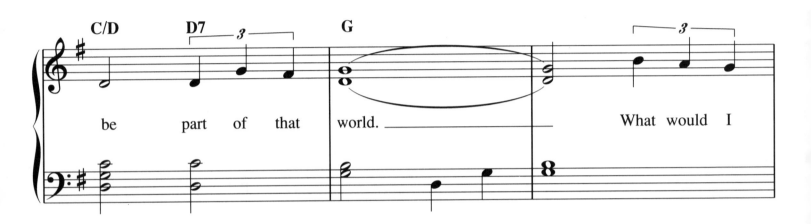

be part of that world. _____ What would I

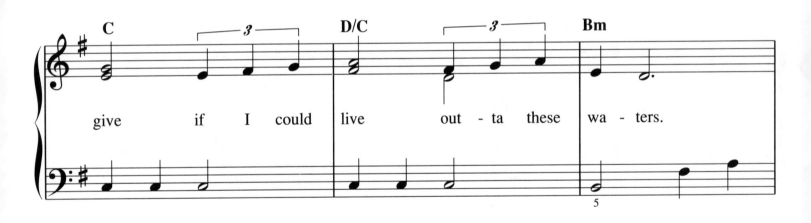

give if I could live out - ta these wa - ters.

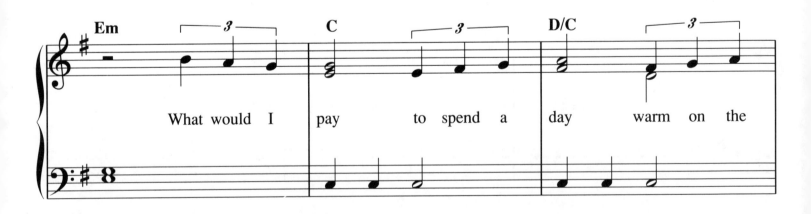

What would I pay to spend a day warm on the

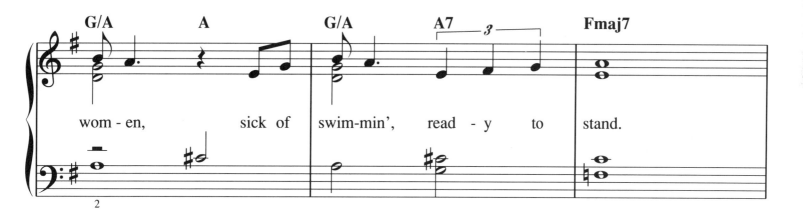

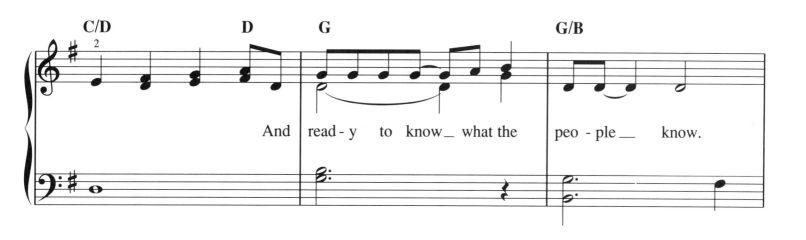

164

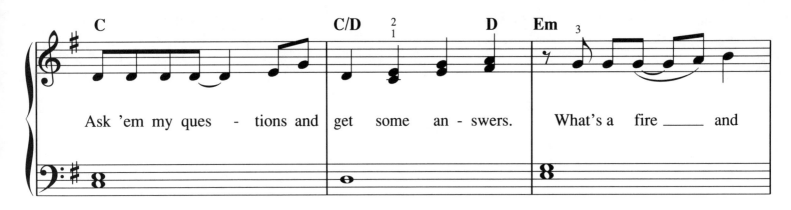

Ask 'em my ques - tions and get some an - swers. What's a fire ____ and

why does it, what's the word, burn. When's it my

turn? Would-n't I love, love to ex - plore that shore up a -

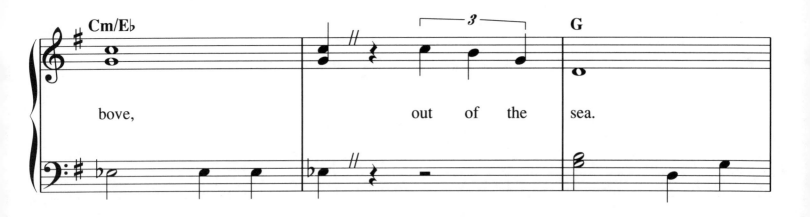

bove, out of the sea.

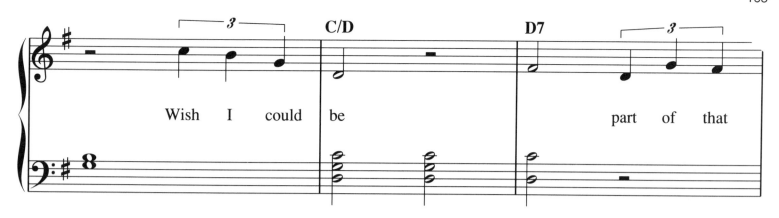

Wish I could be part of that

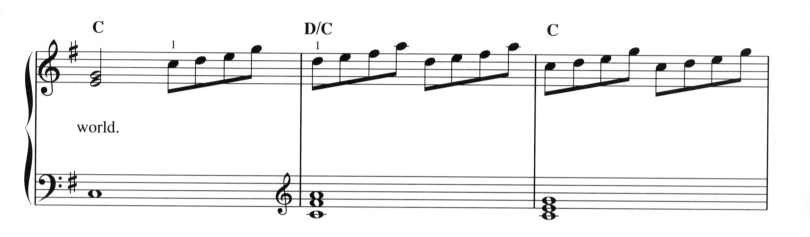

world.

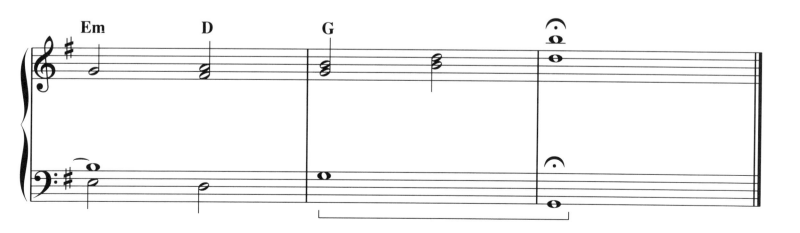

PERFECT ISN'T EASY

from Walt Disney's OLIVER & COMPANY

Words by JACK FELDMAN and BRUCE SUSSMAN
Music by BARRY MANILOW

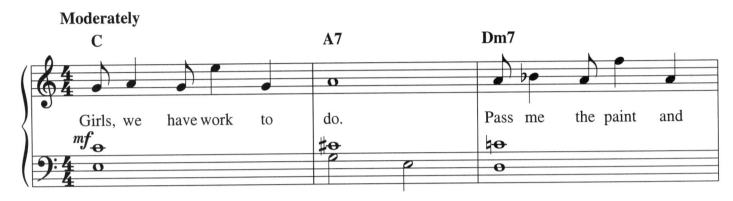

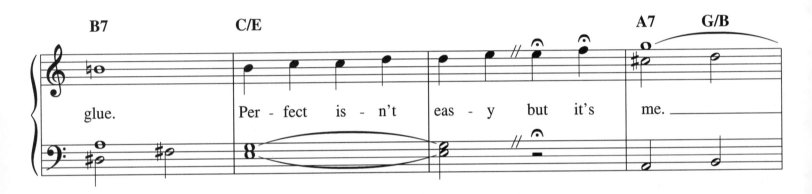

not for my van - i - ty, but for hu - man - i - ty. Each lit - tle step a

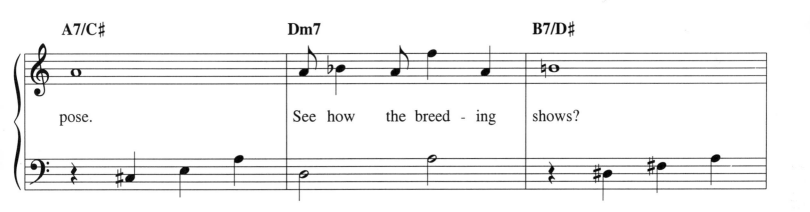

pose. See how the breed - ing shows?

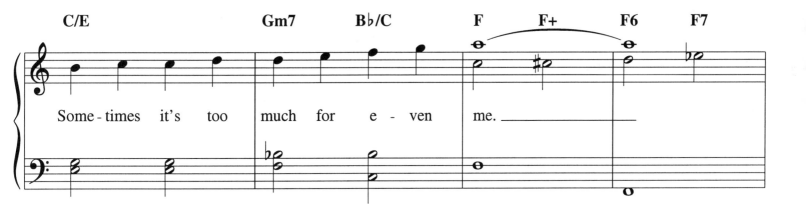

Some - times it's too much for e - ven me. ___

But when all the world says "Yes," __ then who am I to say

168

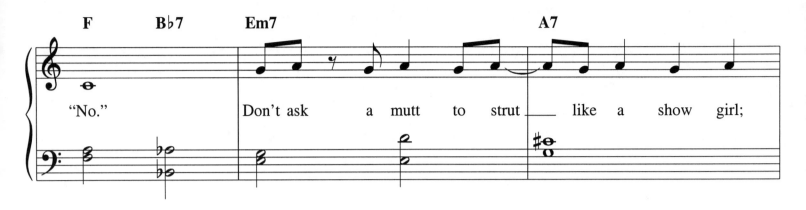

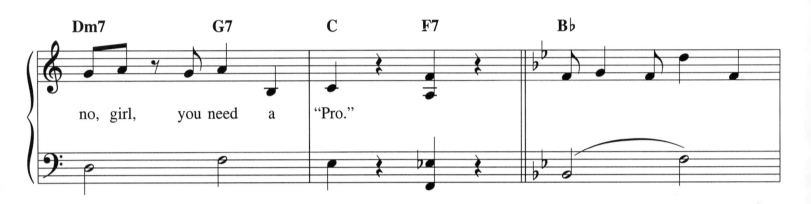

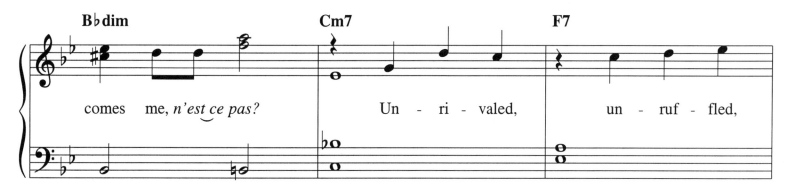

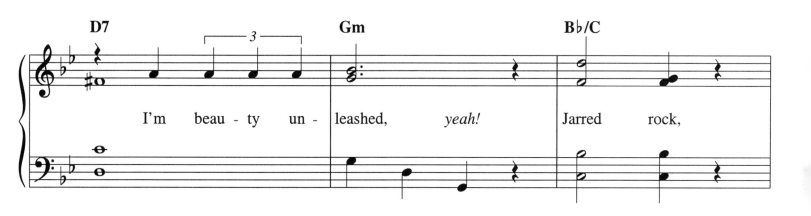

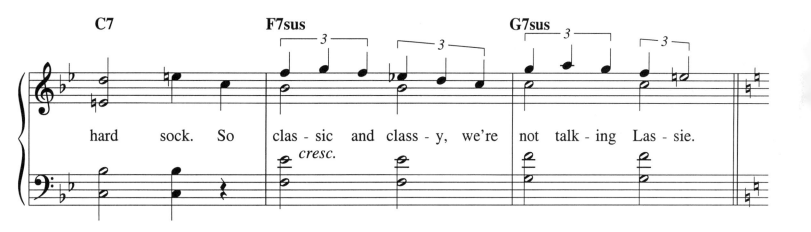

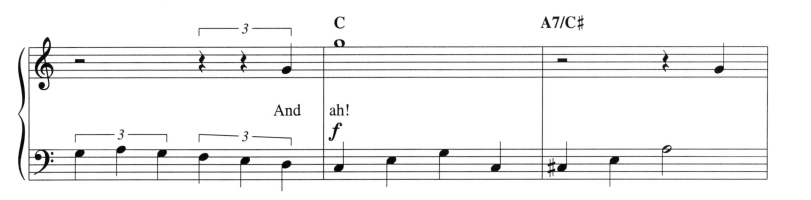

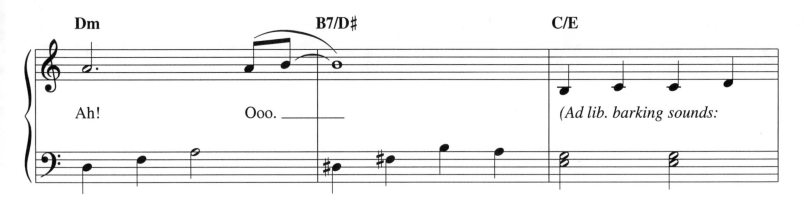

Dm   B7/D♯   C/E

Ah!   Ooo. _____   *(Ad lib. barking sounds:*

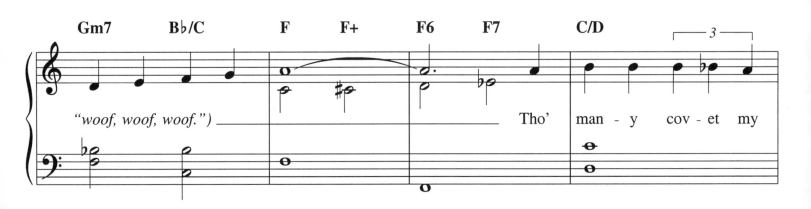

Gm7   B♭/C   F   F+   F6   F7   C/D   3

"woof, woof, woof.") _____ Tho'   man - y   cov - et   my

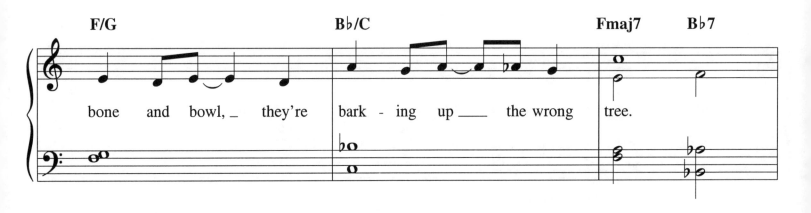

F/G   B♭/C   Fmaj7   B♭7

bone   and   bowl, _ they're   bark - ing   up ___ the wrong   tree.

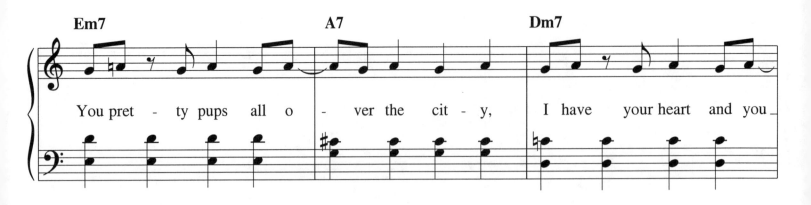

Em7   A7   Dm7

You pret - ty pups all o - ver the cit - y,   I have   your heart   and you _

171

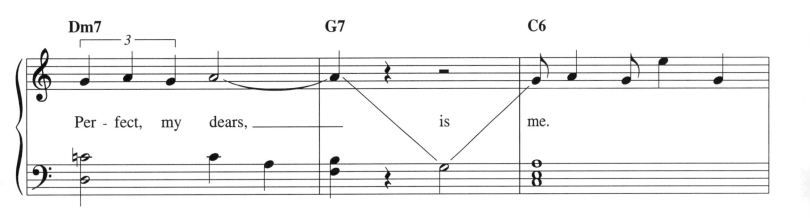

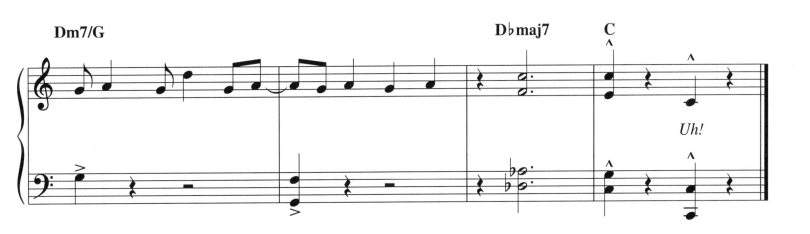

RUMBLY IN MY TUMBLY

from Walt Disney's THE MANY ADVENTURES OF WINNIE THE POOH

Words and Music by RICHARD M. SHERMAN
and ROBERT B. SHERMAN

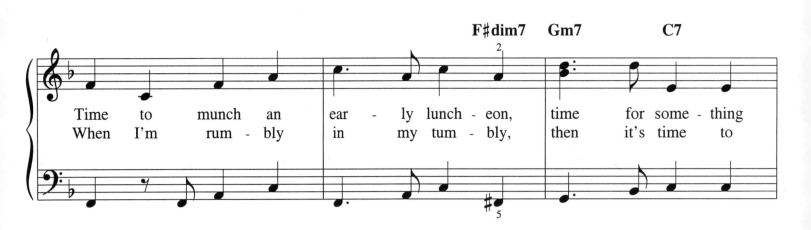

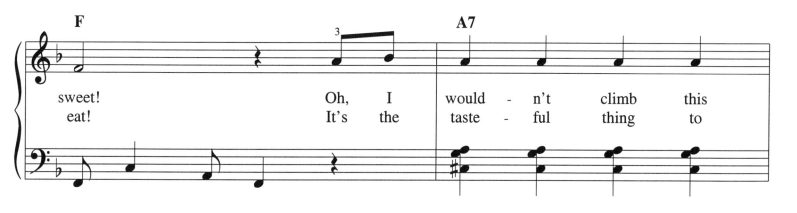

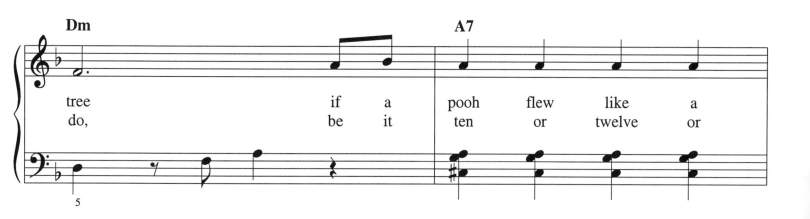

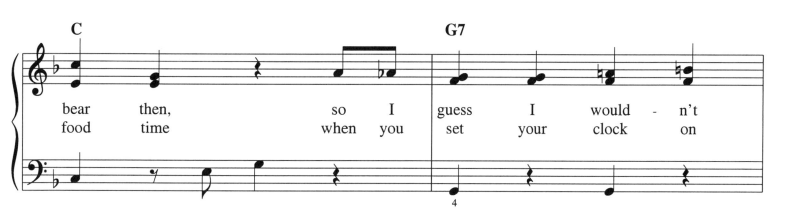

Gm7   C7   F

care then!
pooh time!   Bears love hon-ey and   I'm   a pooh bear,

Gm7   C7   F

so   I do care,   so   I'll climb there.   I'm   so   rum - bly

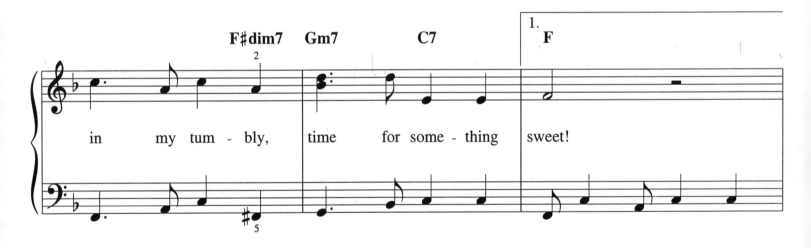

F#dim7   Gm7   C7   1.   F

in   my tum - bly,   time   for some - thing   sweet!

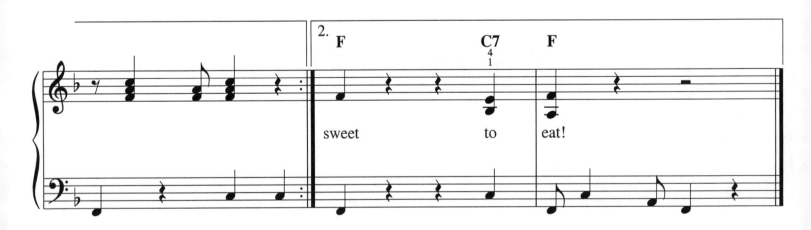

2.   F   C7   F

sweet   to   eat!

A STAR IS BORN

from Walt Disney Pictures' HERCULES

Music by ALAN MENKEN
Lyrics by DAVID ZIPPEL

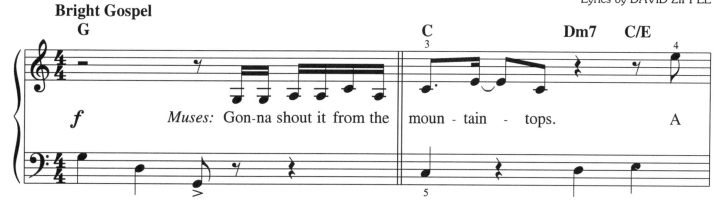

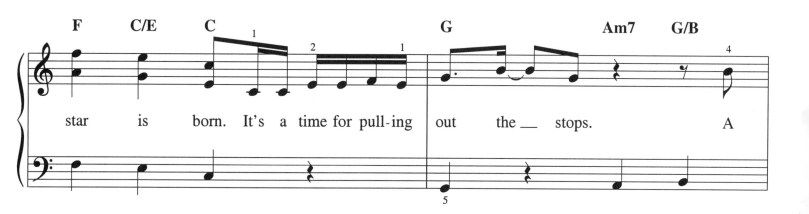

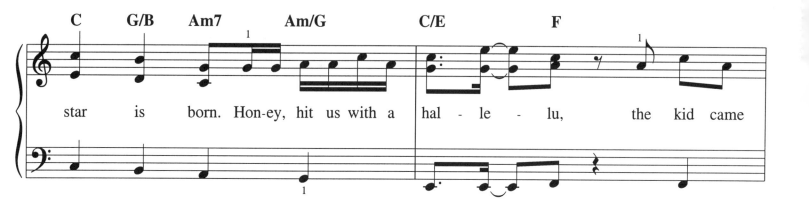

horn, a star is born. He's a he-ro who can

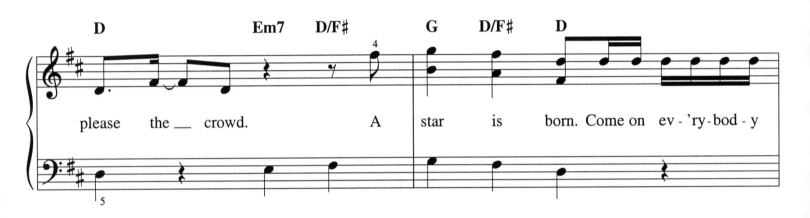

please the __ crowd. A star is born. Come on ev-'ry-bod-y

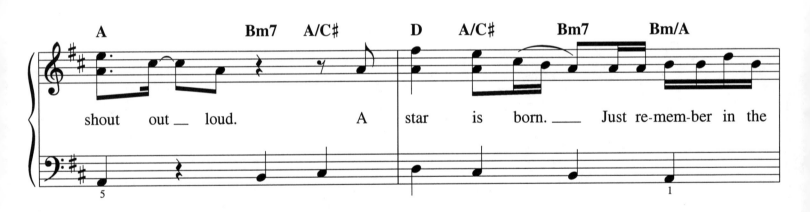

shout out __ loud. A star is born. __ Just re-mem-ber in the

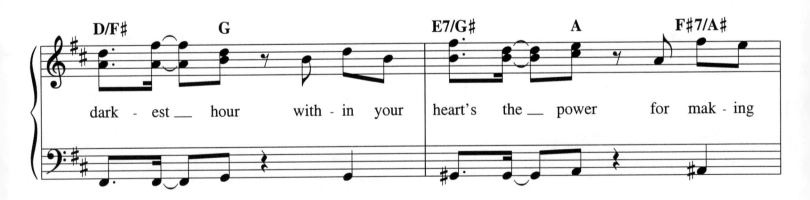

dark - est __ hour with - in your heart's the __ power for mak - ing

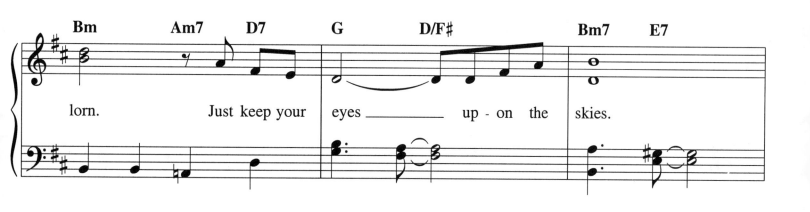

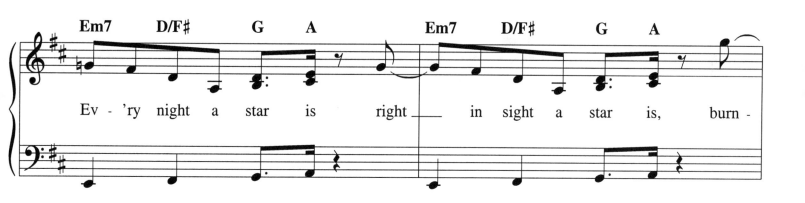

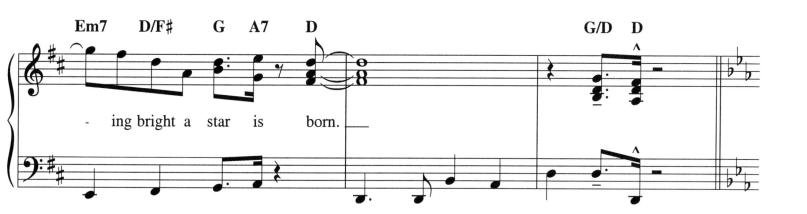

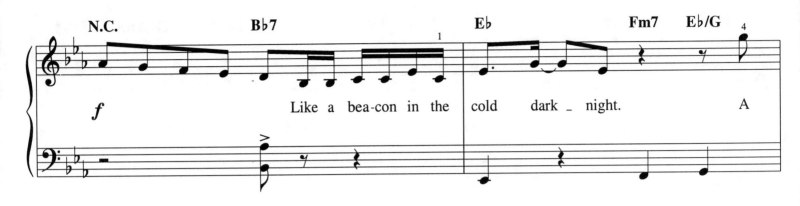

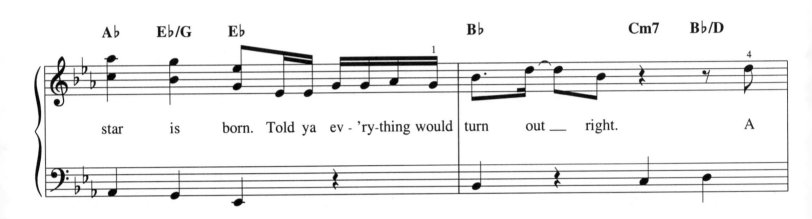

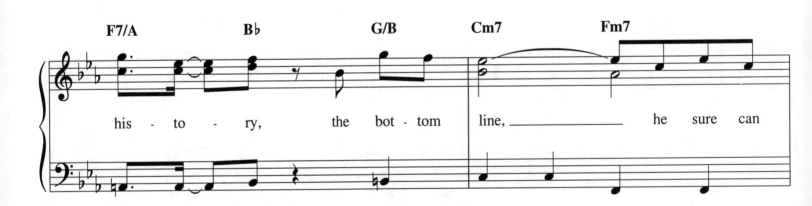

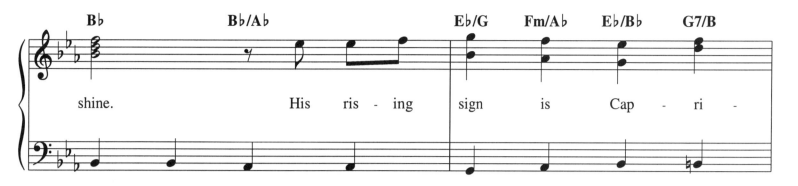

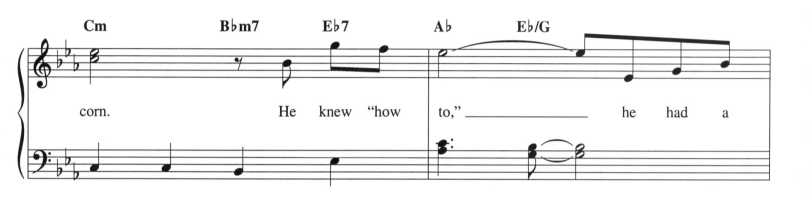

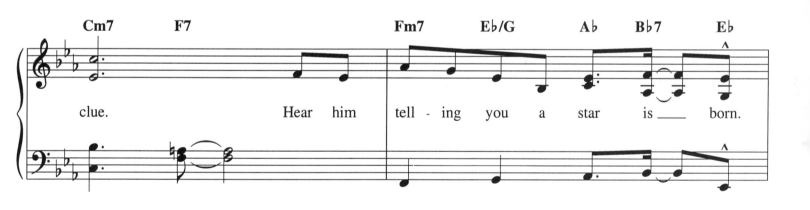

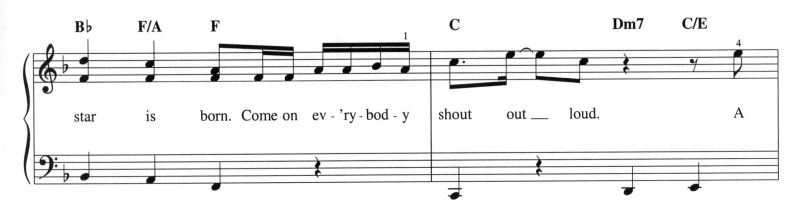

star is born. Come on ev - 'ry - bod - y shout out ___ loud. A

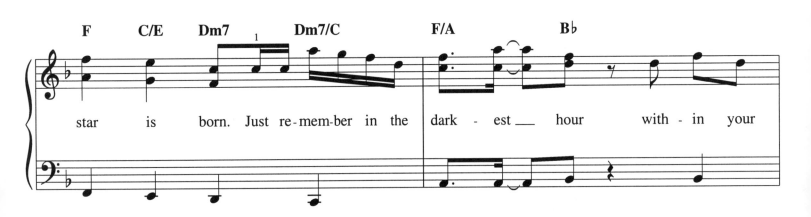

star is born. Just re - mem - ber in the dark - est ___ hour with - in your

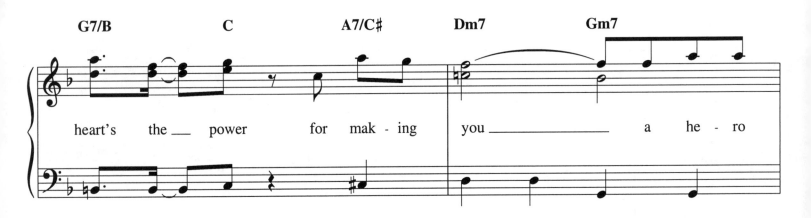

heart's the ___ power for mak - ing you ___ a he - ro

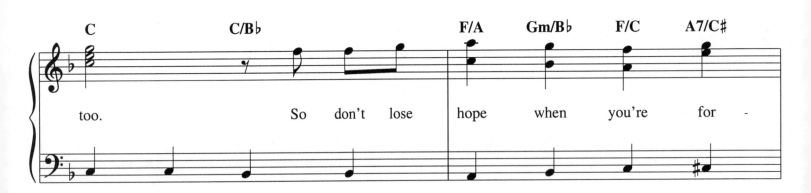

too. So don't lose hope when you're for -

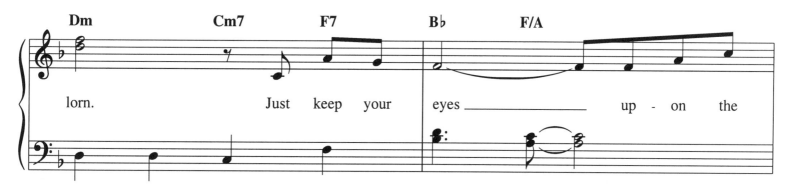

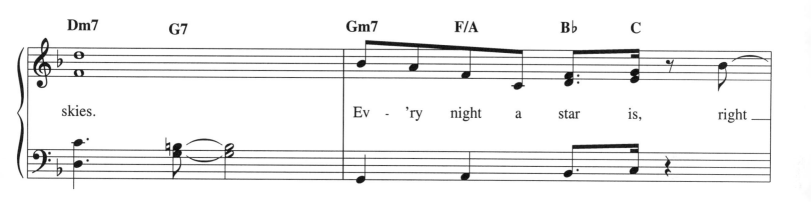

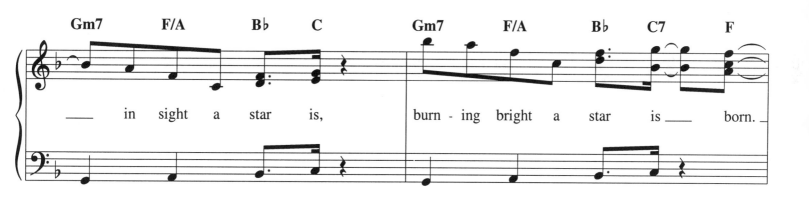

SEIZE THE DAY
from Walt Disney's NEWSIES

Lyrics by JACK FELDMAN
Music by ALAN MENKEN

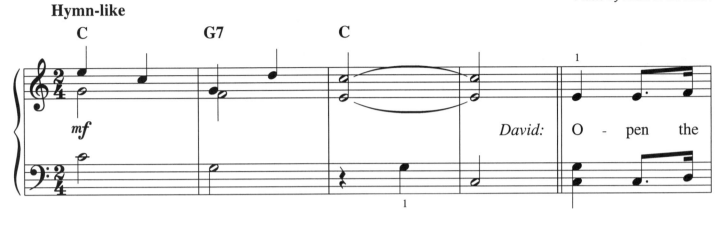

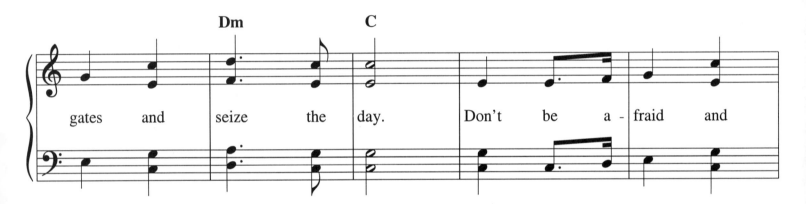

Brightly

day.

David: Now is the time to seize the day.

Newsies: (Now is the time to seize the day.) *David:* Send out the call and join the fray.

Newsies: (Send out the call and join the fray.) *David:* Wrongs will __ be right - ed

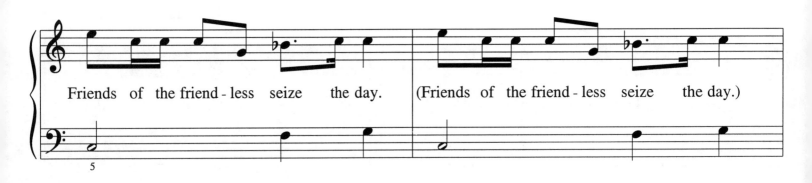

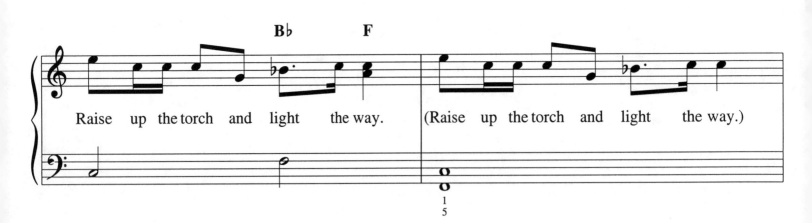

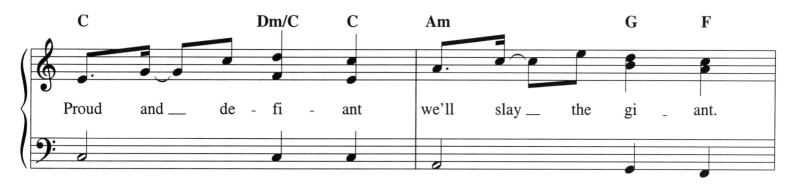

Proud and de - fi - ant we'll slay the gi - ant.

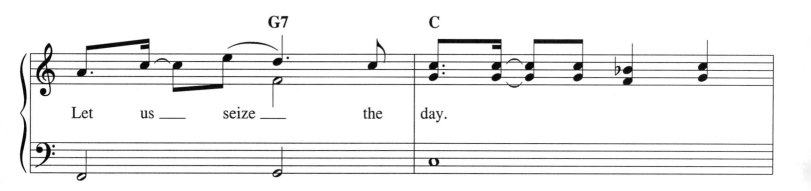

Let us seize the day.

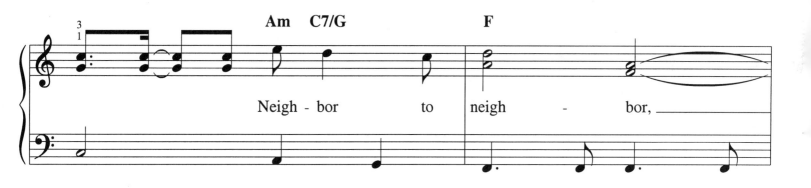

Neigh - bor to neigh - bor,

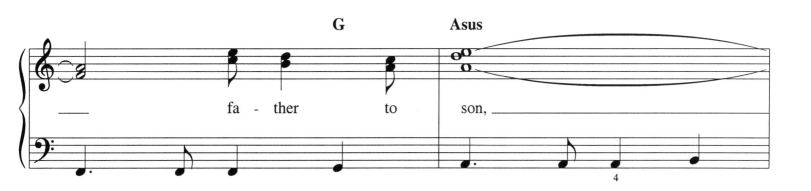

fa - ther to son,

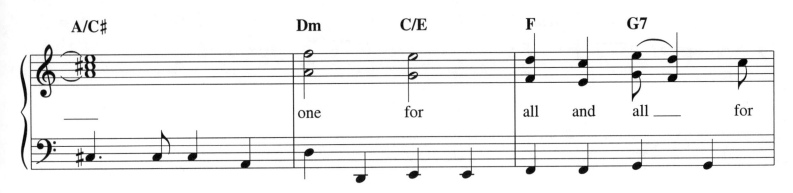

one   for   all   and   all ____   for

one.

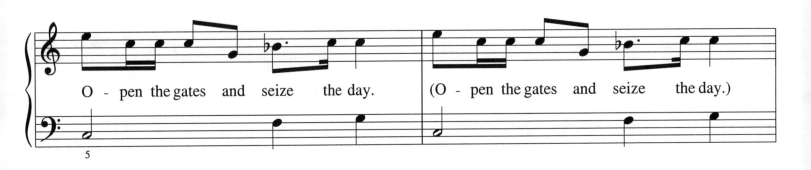

O - pen the gates and seize   the day.   (O - pen the gates and seize   the day.)

Don't be a-fraid and don't de-lay.   (Don't be a-fraid and don't   de-lay.)

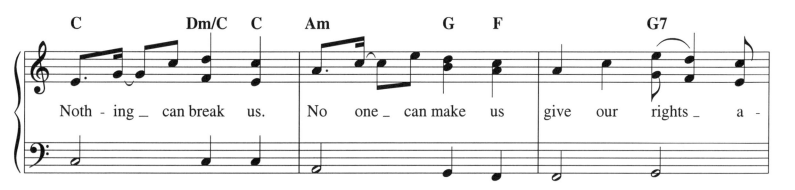

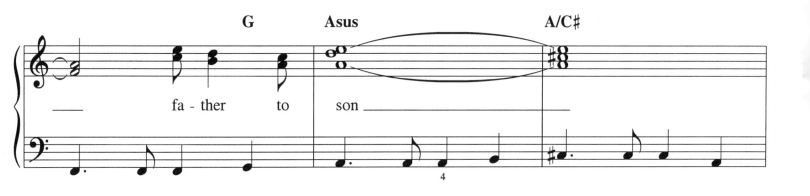

THE SIAMESE CAT SONG
from Walt Disney's LADY AND THE TRAMP

Words and Music by PEGGY LEE
and SONNY BURKE

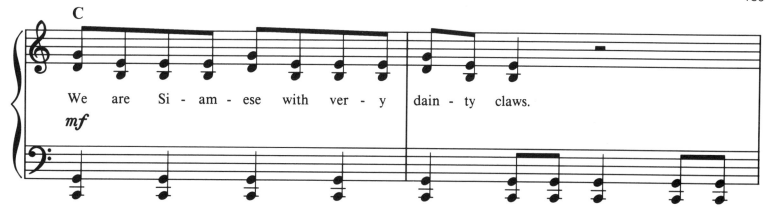

We are Si - am - ese with ver - y dain - ty claws.

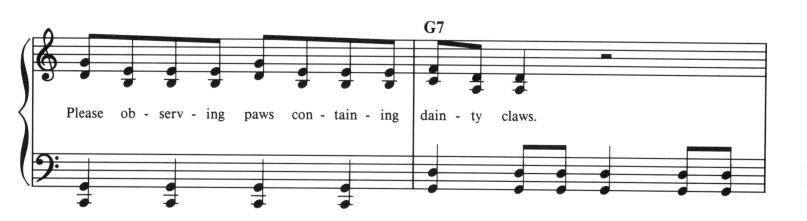

Please ob - serv - ing paws con - tain - ing dain - ty claws.

Now we look-in' o - ver our new dom - i - cile. If we like we stay for may - be

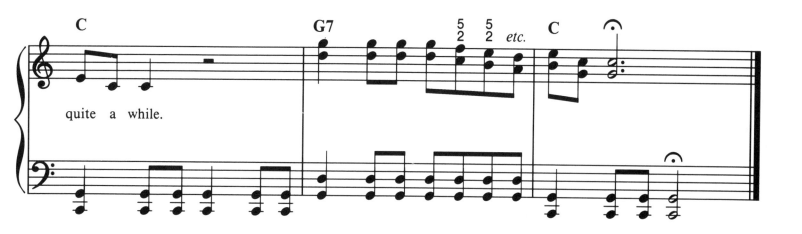

quite a while.

STAY AWAKE
from Walt Disney's MARY POPPINS

Words and Music by RICHARD M. SHERMAN
and ROBERT B. SHERMAN

Slowly and tenderly

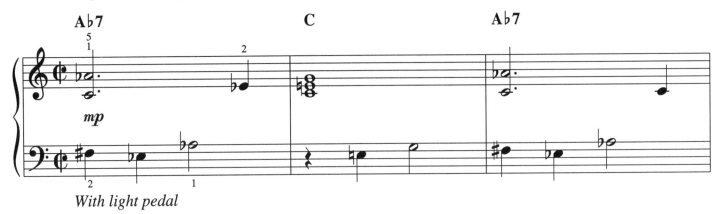

With light pedal

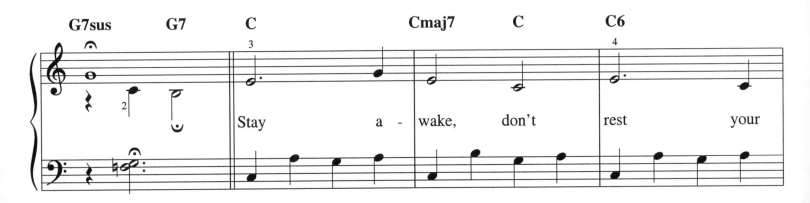

Stay a - wake, don't rest your

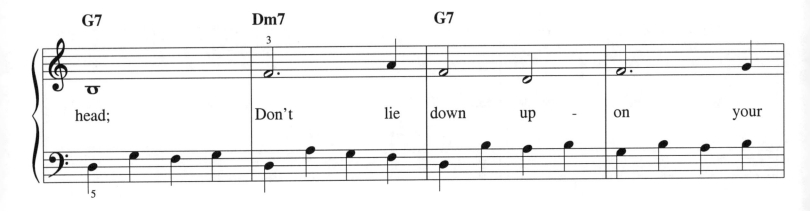

head; Don't lie down up - on your

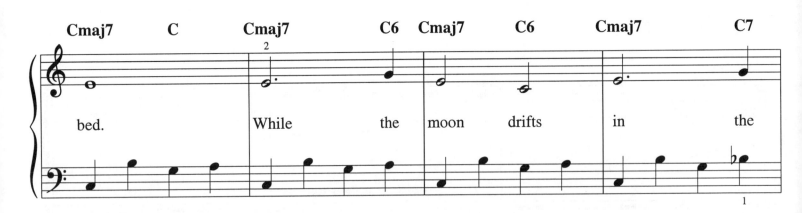

bed. While the moon drifts in the

191

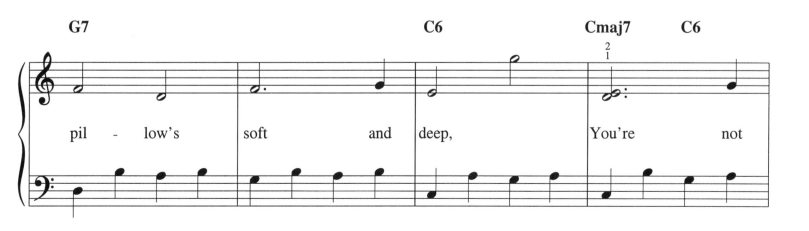

192

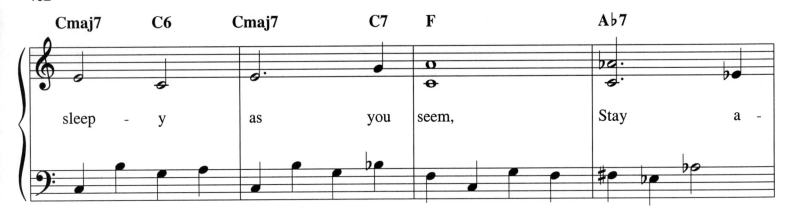

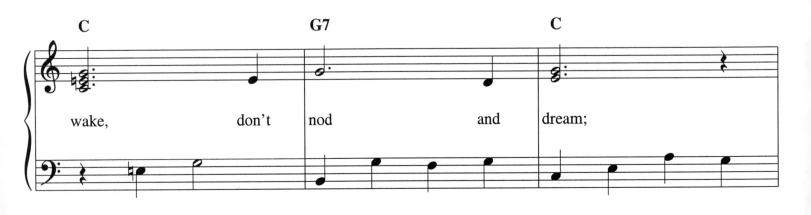

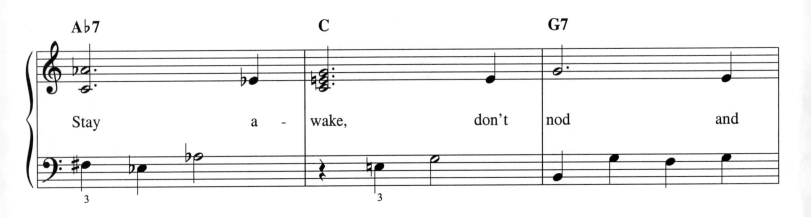

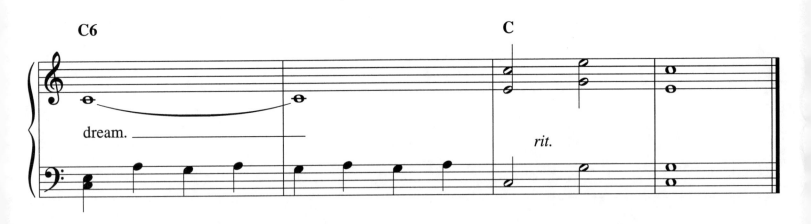

THE UNBIRTHDAY SONG
from Walt Disney's ALICE IN WONDERLAND

Words and Music by MACK DAVID,
AL HOFFMAN and JERRY LIVINGSTON

A ver - y mer - ry un - birth - day to
A ver - y mer - ry un - birth - day to

you,   to you,   a ver - y mer - ry un -
me.   To who?   A ver - y mer - ry un -

birth - day to you,   to you.   It's
birth - day to me.   To you?   Let's

194

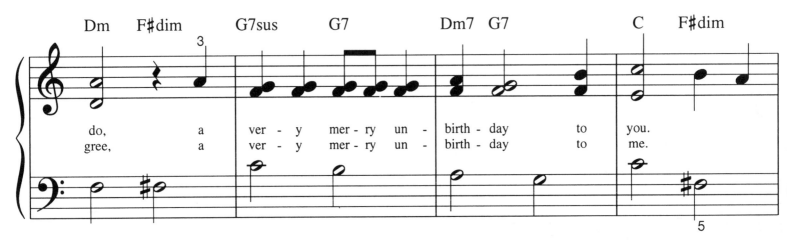

UNDER THE SEA
from Walt Disney's THE LITTLE MERMAID

Lyrics by HOWARD ASHMAN
Music by ALAN MENKEN

The sea - weed is al - ways green - er
Down here__ all the fish is hap - py

in some - bod - y el - se's lake.
as off__ through the waves dey roll.

You dream__ a - bout
The fish__ on the

go - ing up there.
land ain't hap - py.

But that__ is a
They sad__ 'cause they

big mis - take.
in the bowl.

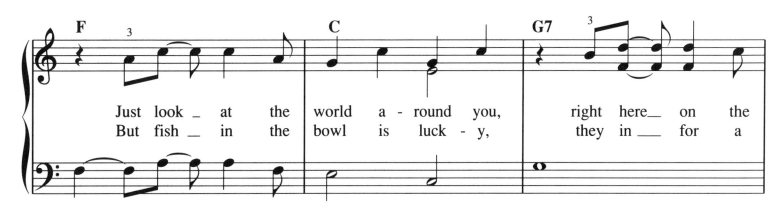

Just look _ at the world a - round you, right here_ on the
But fish _ in the bowl is luck - y, they in ___ for a

o - cean floor. Such won - der - ful things sur - round you.
wors - er fate. One day ___ when the boss get hun - gry

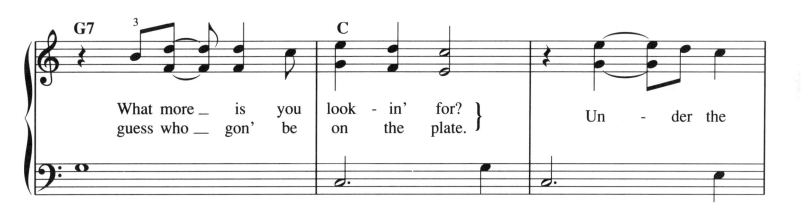

What more _ is you look - in' for? } Un - der the
guess who _ gon' be on the plate.

sea, un - der the sea.

198

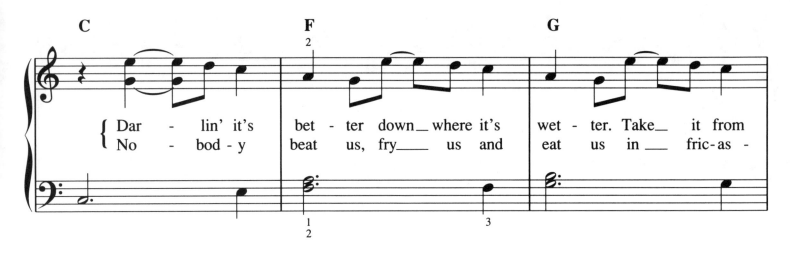

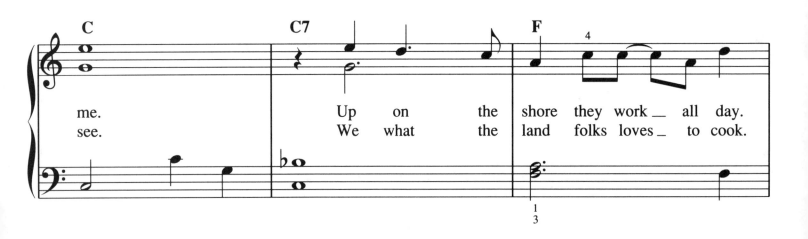

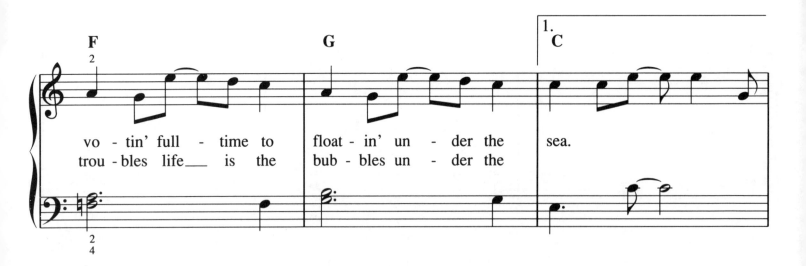

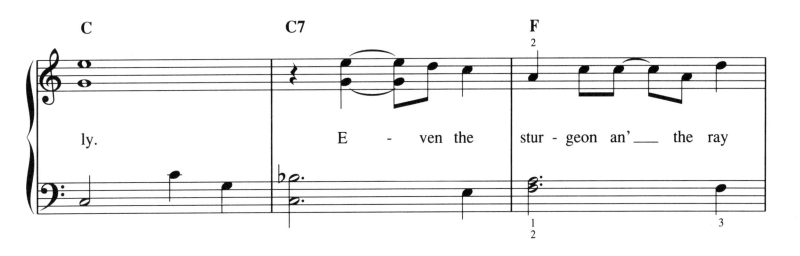

they get the urge 'n' start __ to play. We got the

spir - it, you __ got to hear it un - der the sea.

The newt play the flute. The carp play the harp. The

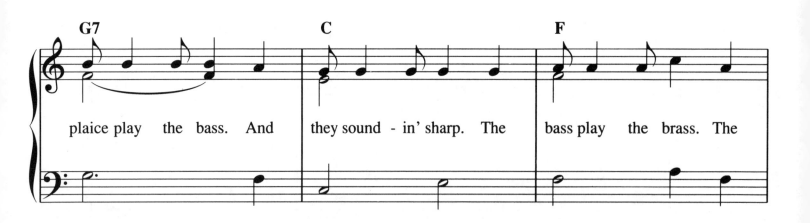

plaice play the bass. And they sound - in' sharp. The bass play the brass. The

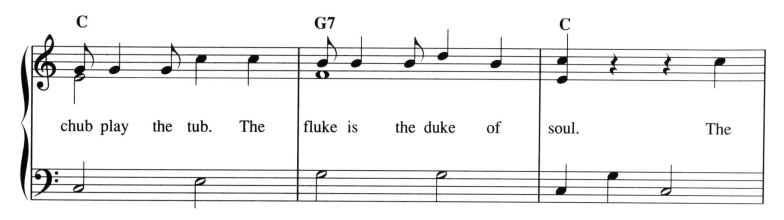

chub play the tub. The fluke is the duke of soul. The

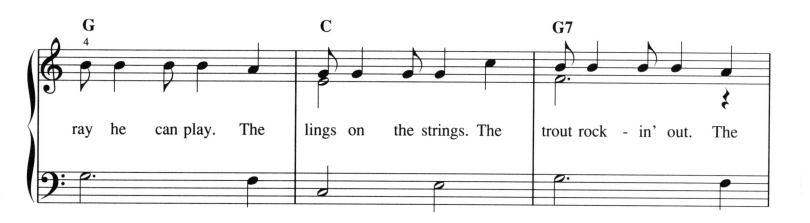

ray he can play. The lings on the strings. The trout rock - in' out. The

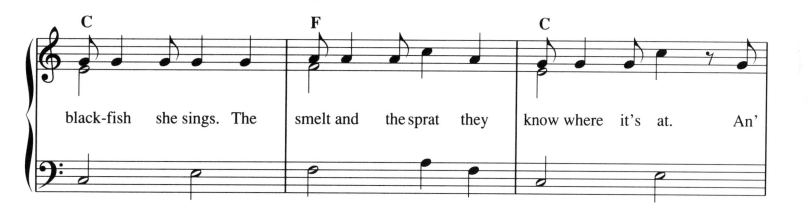

black-fish she sings. The smelt and the sprat they know where it's at. An'

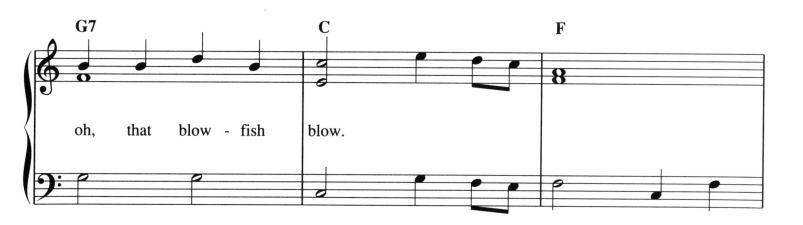

oh, that blow - fish blow.

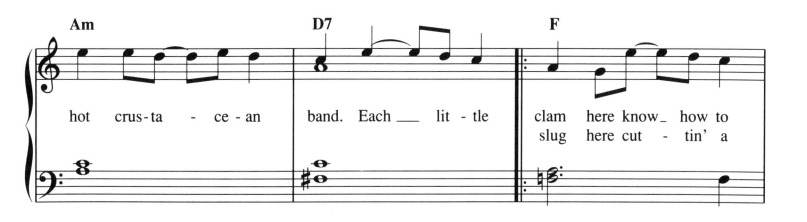

204

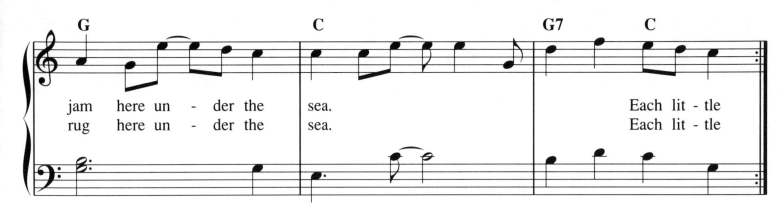

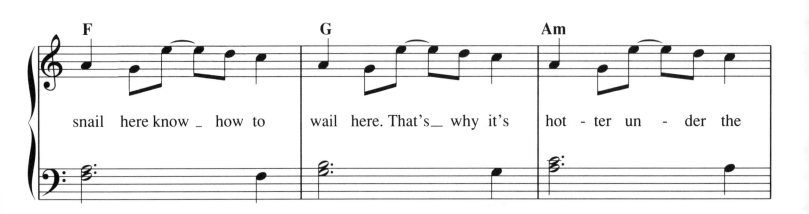

A WHALE OF A TALE

from Walt Disney's 20,000 LEAGUES UNDER THE SEA

Words and Music by NORMAN GIMBEL
and AL HOFFMAN

With a bounce

Got a whale of a tale to tell ya, lads, a

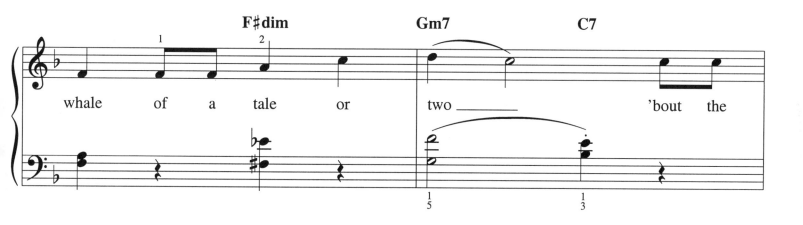

whale of a tale or two 'bout the

flap-pin' fish and the girls I've loved, on nights like this with the

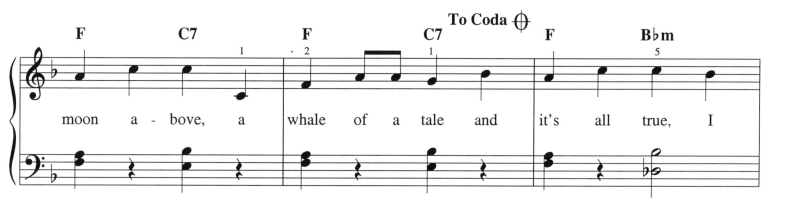

moon a-bove, a whale of a tale and it's all true, I

swear __ by my tat - too.

There was Mer - maid
There was Ty - phoon

Min - nie,
Tes - sie,

met her down in Ma - da - gas - car,
met her on the coast of Ja - va,

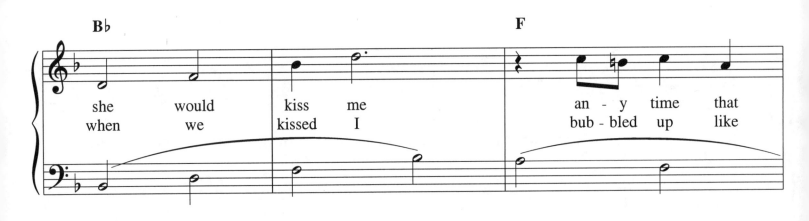

she would
when we

kiss me
kissed I

an - y time that
bub - bled up like

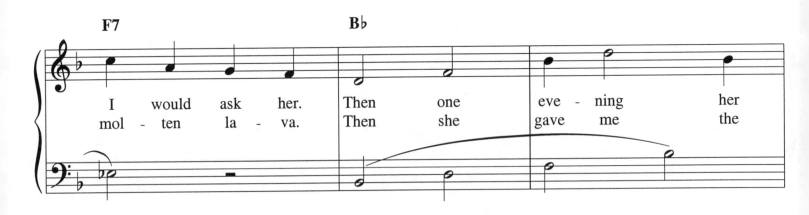

I would ask her.
mol - ten la - va.

Then one
Then she

eve - ning
gave me

her
the

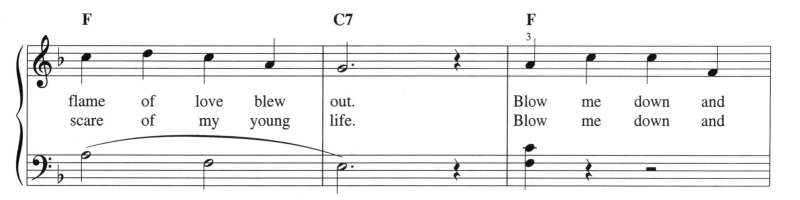

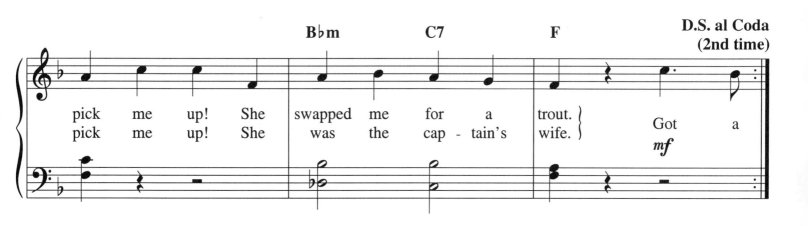

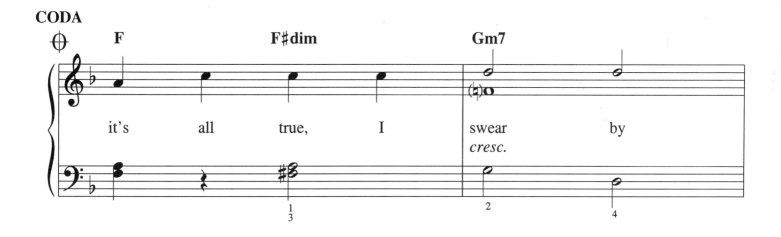

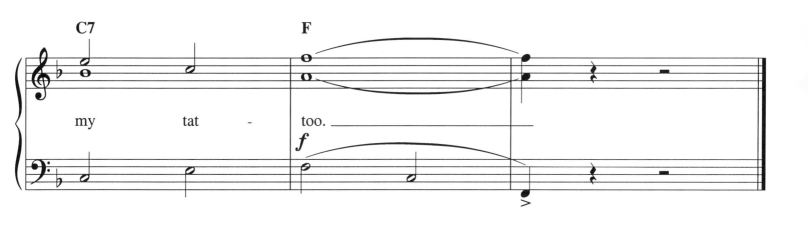

A WHOLE NEW WORLD

from Walt Disney's ALADDIN

Music by ALAN MENKEN
Lyrics by TIM RICE

Slowly and sweetly

Aladdin:

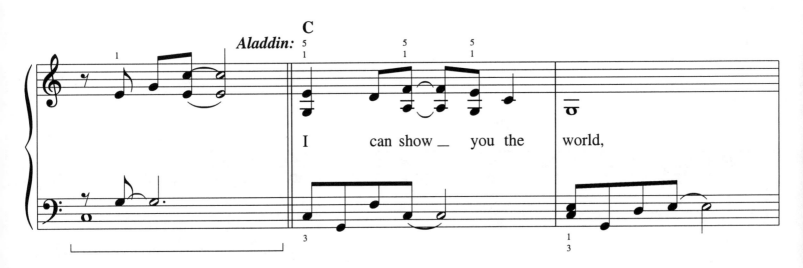

I can show _ you the world,

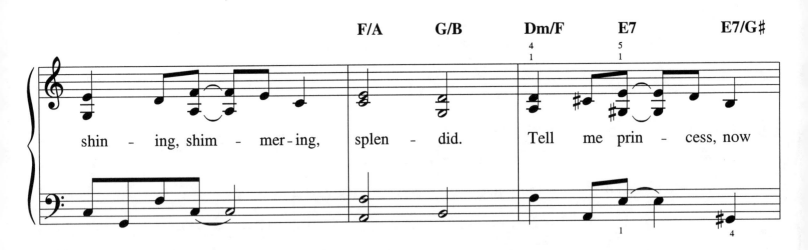

shin - ing, shim - mer-ing, splen - did. Tell me prin - cess, now

when did you last · let your heart ___ de - cide?

I can o - pen your eyes · take you won - der by

won - der · o - ver, side - ways and · un - der on a

mag-ic car - pet ride. · A whole new world

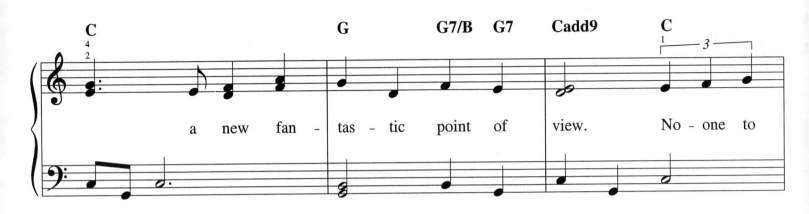

a new fan - tas - tic point of view. No - one to

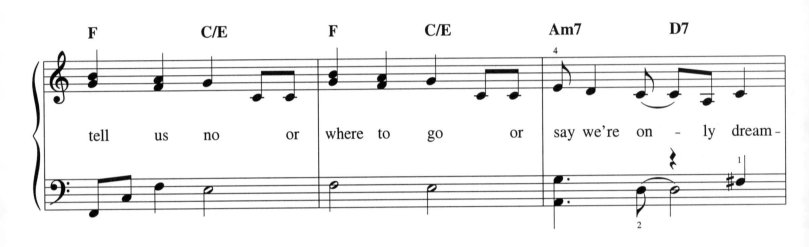

tell us no or where to go or say we're on - ly dream-

Jasmine:

ing. A whole new world a daz - zling

place I nev - er knew. But when I'm way up here it's

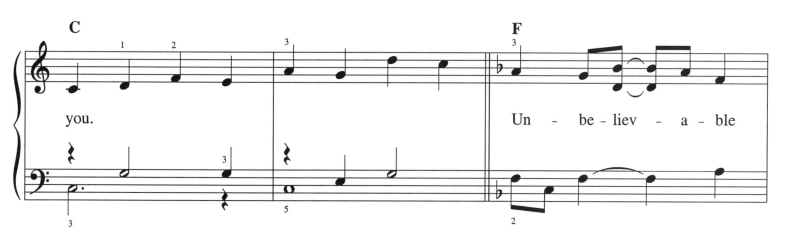

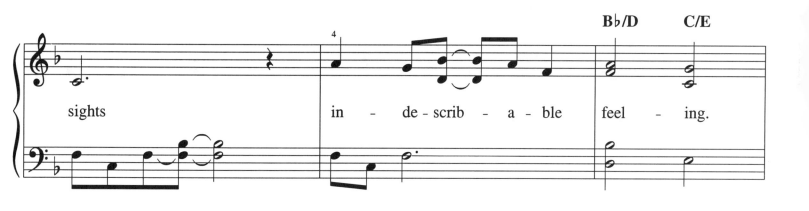

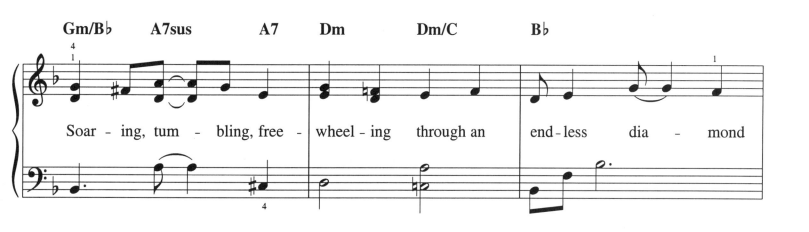

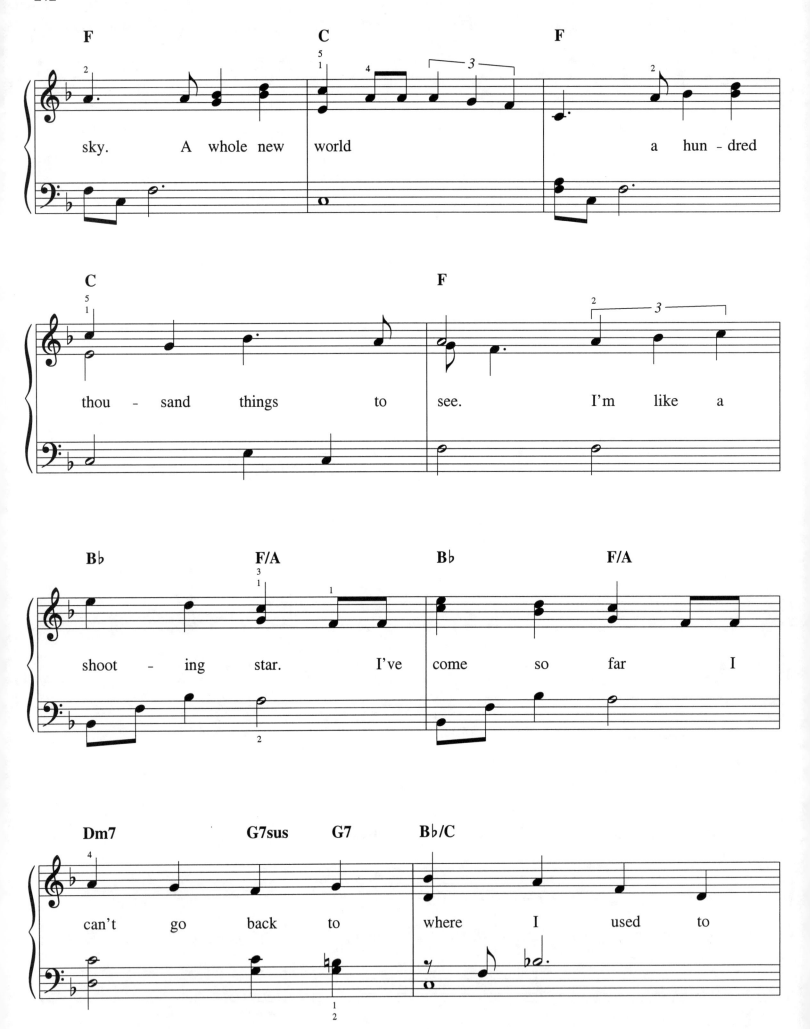

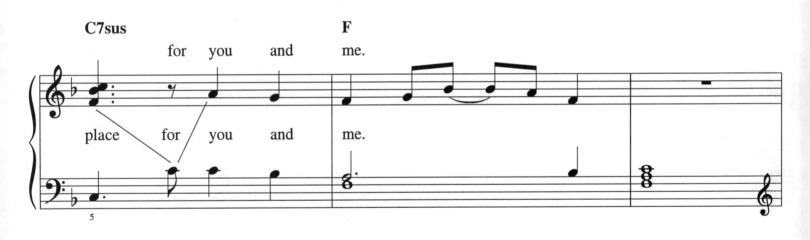

WINNIE THE POOH
from Walt Disney's THE MANY ADVENTURES OF WINNIE THE POOH

Words and Music by RICHARD M. SHERMAN
and ROBERT B. SHERMAN

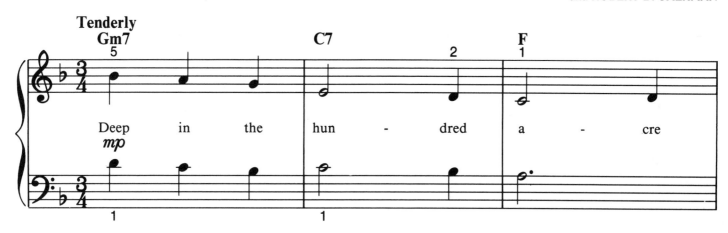

Deep in the hun - dred a - cre

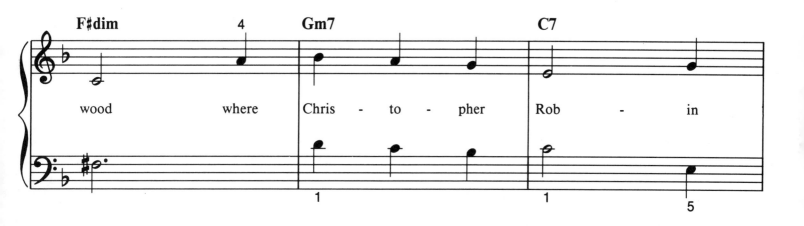

wood where Chris - to - pher Rob - in

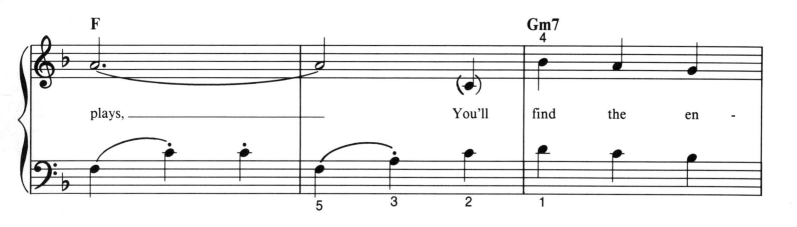

plays, You'll find the en -

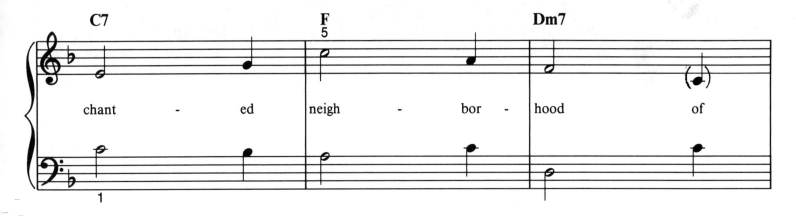

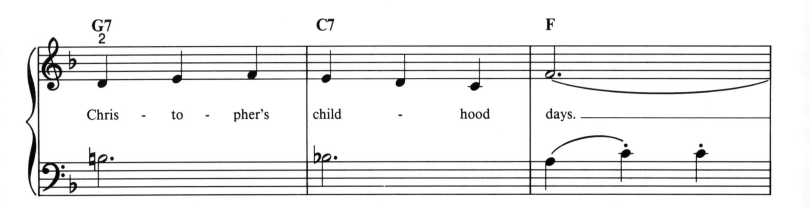

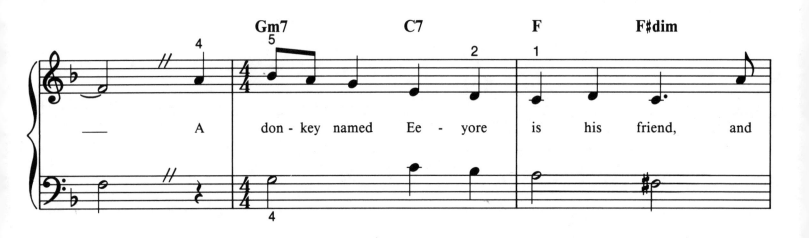

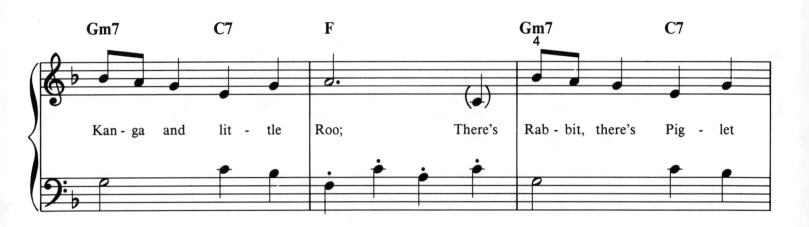

YOU'VE GOT A FRIEND IN ME

from Walt Disney's TOY STORY

Music and Lyrics by
RANDY NEWMAN

You've got a friend in me.
You've got a friend in me.

You've got a friend in me.
You've got a friend in me.

When the road looks
You got troubles, then

rough a-head ___ and you're
I got 'em too. ___

miles ___ and miles ___ from your
There is-n't an - y - thing

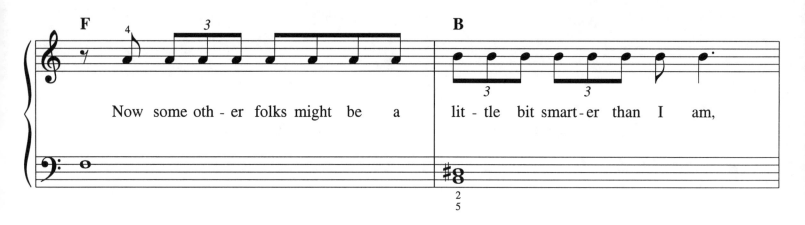

Now some oth - er folks might be a lit - tle bit smart - er than I am,

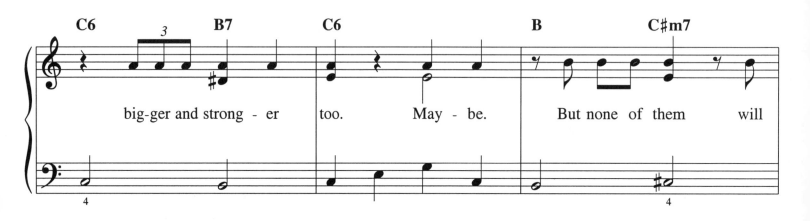

big-ger and strong - er too. May - be. But none of them will

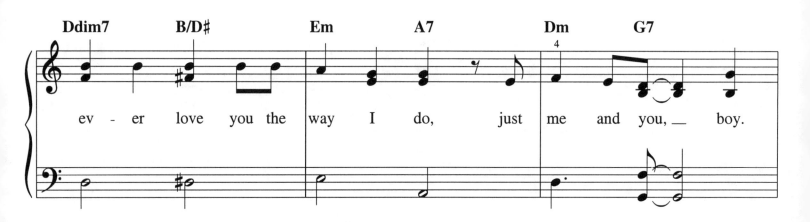

ev - er love you the way I do, just me and you, __ boy.

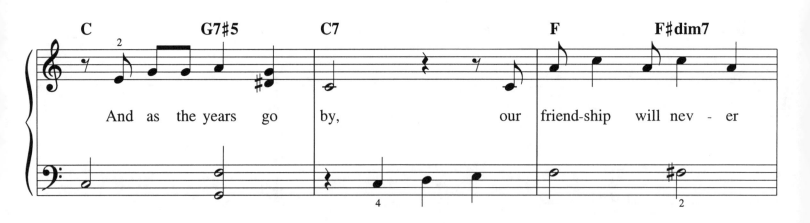

And as the years go by, our friend-ship will nev - er

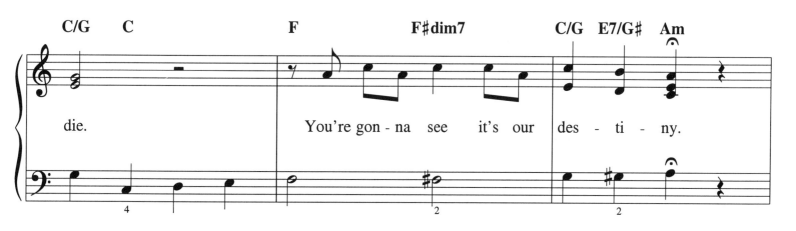

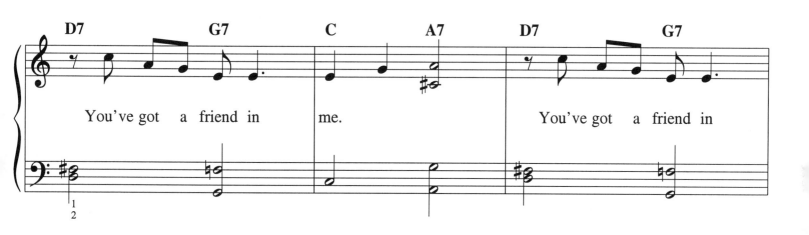

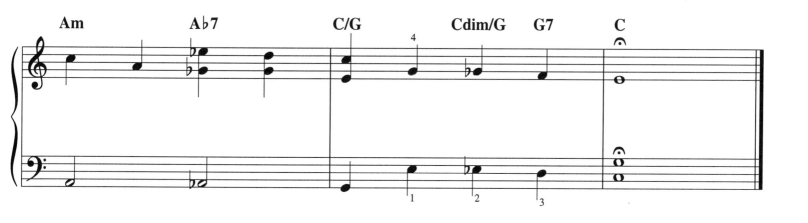

THE WORK SONG
from Walt Disney's CINDERELLA

Words and Music by MACK DAVID,
AL HOFFMAN and JERRY LIVINGSTON

Brightly

Cin- der- el- la, Cin- der- el- la, All I hear is Cin- der-

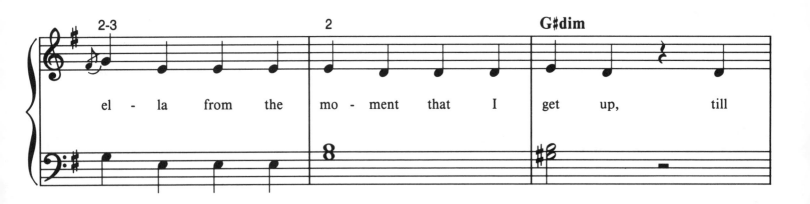

el- la from the mo- ment that I get up, till

shades of night are fall- ing. There is- n't an- y let up, I

hear them call- ing, call- ing, "Go up and do the at- tic and go

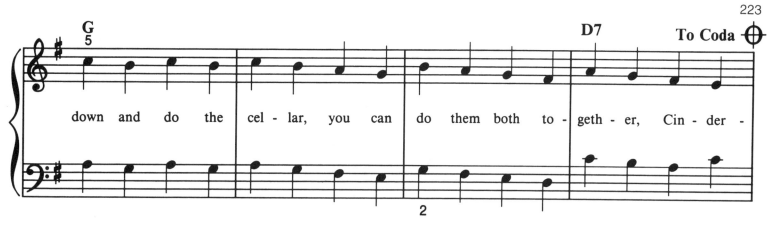

down and do the cel - lar, you can do them both to - geth - er, Cin - der -

el - la." Cin - der - How love - ly

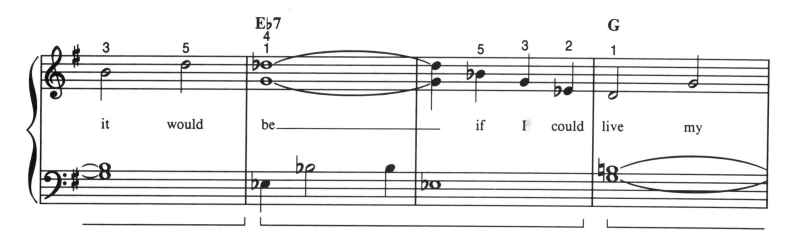

it would be if I could live my

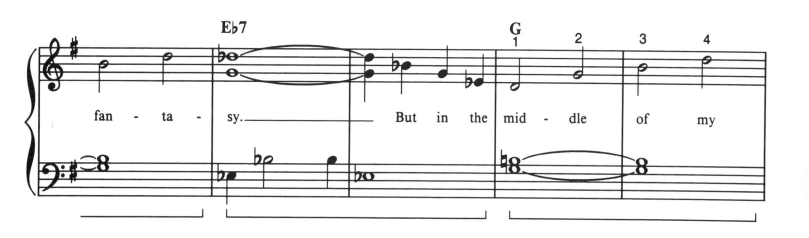

fan - ta - sy. But in the mid - dle of my

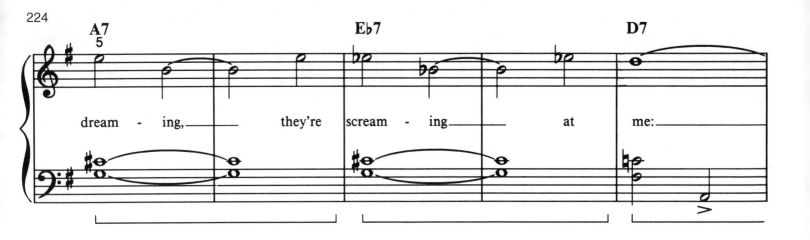

dream - ing,_____ they're scream - ing_____ at me:_____

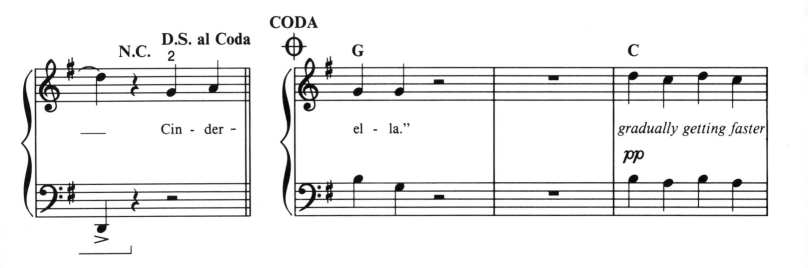

_____ Cin - der-

CODA

el - la."

gradually getting faster

pp

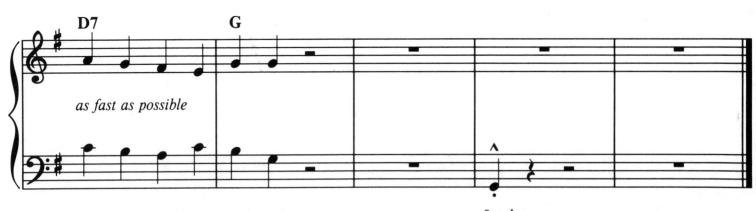

as fast as possible

8va lower